God, You Can Take My Mental Illness –

Just Not The Part Where You Speak To Me

© *Jo Hilder 2012*

Acknowledgements

For Ben – the most faithful and gentle man I have ever known.

Thank you

Sherwood Cliffs Christian Community –

for giving me back the husband of my youth.

Paul Macklin and Michelle Falzon –

for believing in my art and telling me the truth.

Abigail Westbrook of ASourceOfJoy Graphic Design –

for the cover artwork.

Helen Esteban - for confectionary reconnaissance. ☺

Burnside Writers Collective - for introducing me to a supportive, creative

tribe of writers, and a supportive, symbiotic tribe of readers.

My family - for your love.

And especially, to all my readers - for your support.

Really nice things people were not paid to say about me.

"With haunting and hilarious honesty, Jo Hilder can be as reflective as Henri Nouwen, as bold as Anne Lamott, and as thunderous as fellow Aussies AC/DC. Jo's inspiring faith journey is truly high voltage."

Bert Montgomery, writer/teacher/minister
Psychic Pancakes & Communion Pizza
Elvis, Willie, Jesus & Me
www.bertmontgomery.com

"Jo Hilder is a refreshing and authentic writer who draws you into the intimacies of her life. A fantastic read with laugh-out-loud humor scattered throughout, 'God, You Can Take My Mental Illness' is a great collection of personal essays. Jo confronts myth after myth of what the Christian life is supposed to look like. Marriage, mental health and alcoholism are themes she visits often, but it is threaded together with faith, hope and love. This book will provide readers reassurance that God is not looking for perfect lives...just honest ones."

Pam Hogeweide, author
Unladylike: Resisting the Injustice of Inequality in the Church
http://www.pamhogeweide.com/

"The only way I know of to develop a writing voice worth sharing is to become a person who has weathered a great storm well. Jo has weathered more than her share and the result is beautiful. Surviving cancer and marital difficulties has left Jo a witty, gritty, and fearless writer. Reading Jo's work makes me laugh, think, and get angry. She makes me *feel*, which just might be the greatest gift a writer can share."

Larry Shallenberger, pastor and author
Divine Intention: How God's Work in the Early Church Empowers Us Today. larryshallenberger.com

"Jo's voice is exactly what the Christian world needs right now - unabashed, unashamed, and uninhibited. Jo's work has become essential at Burnside Writer's Collective, where her authentic, relatable voice prods readers to push the envelope of their spiritual experience and break into a new kind of being."

Kim Gottschild - Associate Editor, Burnside Writer's Collective
Cupcake Countenance Columnist
Burnside Writers Collective
http://burnsidewriters.com/

"What I like most about Jo's writing is that she is not afraid to ponder the hard questions. A Christian for many years, she doesn't write 'nice religious fluff' – her work is gutsy, down-to-earth, warts-and-all – but most of all it's 'real', and for that reason, the reader is able to relate in a practical way. Jo has experienced much in her life – cancer, mental illness, marriage breakdown and reconciliation, an alcoholic husband, and she has been involved in many facets of ministry. She is to be applauded for sharing so honestly and willingly to encourage others. She's funny, she's quirky, she's passionate, she's witty, she's relevant – and I'm addicted to her blog!"

Janet Camilleri, editor/founder/president
Footprints Magazine
Footprints Women's Ministries Inc. (Australia)
http://www.footprintsaustralia.com/

"Jo Hilder is cantankerous, opinionated, objectionable, tough, courageous, raw, vulnerable, insightful and above all daringly honest. Just the qualities needed in one who confront emperors inside and outside of the Church and point to their nakedness. When other people pretend that the tough issues can be glossed over or treated with simplistic doctrine, Jo points to the fact that there's a complicated elephant in the room that can't be ignored. Never one to blindly follow the crowd or to regurgitate someone else's teaching, Jo's ideas stem from her breadth of life experience, depth of original insights and her courageous capacity to be true to herself and tell it exactly as she sees it. Should I ever act like a naked emperor I'll look to Jo to recommend an honest tailor."

Paul Macklin – Director, Amazing People
http://www.amazingpeople.com.au/

"She writes in an irreverent and hilarious voice that is imbued with truth, simplicity, and love. I've recommended her blog and specific posts to countless friends looking for non-traditional axioms about faith and life.

Elysha O'Brien, Ph.D.
Wet Clay Blog
http://www.elysha23.wordpress.com

"Before you read this, I want you to know that I think you should like Jo Hilder because she's Australian. Australians are the best, what with their different slang and their summers being in the winter. But I bet that once you start reading, you'll end up liking Jo because her writing is incisive, witty, and, most importantly, very, very honest."

Jordan Green, Editor-in-chief
Burnside Writers Collective

Table of Contents

God You Can Take My Mental Illness –

Just Not The Part Where You Speak To Me.

Introduction

Firstly, I just want to thank you for choosing to read a book with such a wordy title. I promise to try and make everything else from now on far more succinct. This book is lovingly named after a recent blog post I wrote called *God Can Take My Mental Illness, Just Not The Part Where He Speaks To Me,* which appears here as the very last chapter. I thought the title, wordy as it is, might do perfectly for this book, made up as it is mainly of essays and stories about either my own mental illnesses, or those of the people I know, and also about my job as a mental health support worker over the past twelve months.

I will clarify now that I do actually believe in God, so the title of the book may bear either more or less irony considering what you think about that. I met God as a very young girl after He started visiting me in my room at night for long chats. *Yes, I know how that sounds.* Later on, I aligned myself with evangelical Christianity, becoming "born-again" when aged thirteen at a high school Bible study. Incidentally, I'm the only person who believes in God in my immediate family of origin. But despite this, and the fact I've been in the past diagnosed as mentally ill, *and* everything else that's happened to me even since I became a Christian, I've never doubted God is anything other than absolutely real.

I was a troubled teenager. I first went to see a psychologist when I was in my teens, though not specifically about the believing in God thing. My mother thought I should go and *talk to someone*, which is a nice way of saying *I love you, but I'm fairly certain you need some professional psychological help*. It's true my family were baffled by my faith in God, but probably no more so than by a lot of other things I did and said. I was overwhelmed periodically with symptoms of anxiety, as well as with obsessive and depressive thoughts. I vacillated between blaming either my family (*didn't understand me*) or the church (*always trying to change me*) for my issues, but ended up clinging to both for dear life when I had my first baby, unmarried and chronically ill with Epstein-Barr, two months after I turned twenty. I look back now at the confused, muddled mess of a girl I was, desperately trying to get my needs met, needs I couldn't even name, with a sense of deep compassion. No wonder a Jesus who saves appealed to me – if I needed anything, I needed *saving,* even if it was just from the consequences of my own actions.

All things considered, it's my husband Ben who has turned out to be the real hero of the piece. After fathering our first baby at the age of eighteen during a short-lived foray away from his firm Pentecostal Christian upbringing, he married me with no idea what on earth he was getting himself into. My parents tried to talk him out of it, bless them. I now know that when it comes to the trials of marriage, there's faithful, and then there's *faithful*. It's only now, twenty or so years later, when we have sons the same age as their father was when he married me than I can defer to my husband with the respect he so truly deserves. I write more about our early years, and about the way the church behaved towards us in *Why Christians Are Not The Boss Of Marriage.*

When the church tells young people that getting married means they won't be living in sin any more, they are telling a big fat lie. I got married a sinner, and I stayed one, because I'm pretty sure that hoping your husband will fall under a bus on his way home from work is as big a sin as sleeping with him when he wasn't your husband. I was not a very good Christian wife at first, but I gave it a red-hot go, gradually improving over time. But it wasn't easy. With a young family on our hands we both had to grow up very quickly. The one good thing about getting your husband straight out of his childhood home is you get to train him up just the way you like him, and once Ben was old enough to grow a full beard, he was very well trained indeed. *And much, much wiser.* It was after the birth of our fourth child that I was properly diagnosed with both post-natal depression and bipolar disorder (formerly known as manic depression). I'd probably had

PND after the births of all our children. A formal diagnosis and deeper understanding of my sporadic and sometimes illogical thoughts, moods and behaviors certainly has helped a lot in managing my moods, particularly the depression part. But if Ben and I thought a few early marriage hiccups and my being diagnosed with a little ole mental illness were the worst things that could happen to us, we were in for a nasty shock.

In 2003, after seven months of being shooed away by the family doctor and told nothing was wrong with me, I was hospitalised and diagnosed with stage 3 Non-Hodgkin's Lymphoma. Three months of chemotherapy and two of radiotherapy ensued, and were successful in bringing the cancer under control. But alarmingly, after I was well into remission and the crisis had passed I began having random panic attacks. Coincidentally, this started happening right about the time Ben came clean about his having become an alcoholic in the period while we were getting our heads around my not having died of cancer. For some reason, we were both too busy to even notice.

Over a period of about twelve months, Ben experienced an emotional and mental breakdown in slow, painful increments. His business went broke. Our twenty-year marriage disintegrated, and he was admitted to a residential Christian drug and alcohol rehabilitation program in June 2009. I was now a middle-aged single mother with appalling bone density, absolutely no money, a nasty penchant for panic attacks and an alcoholic, soon-to-be-ex-husband. Unfortunately, the church seemed to want to pretend Ben had never actually existed in the first place, and the Christian school wrote and demanded I settle accounts immediately or remove our children forthwith. We learned a lot about compassion, mercy and grace in that time. I revisit some of it in *From Burial to Banqueting Table.*

Through it all, perhaps even in spite of it, Ben and I clutched manfully to our Christianity like a man overboard to a piece of shattered hull. Our questions about how *these kinds of things can happen, even when you pray every day and ask God very nicely could nothing bad please happen, thank you* went unanswered by the church, perhaps because they simply didn't have a clue. Understandably, many of our own formerly non-negotiable expectations and beliefs were challenged, and even changed. We questioned God's ability to always control, and always manage to keep His good reputation despite, the sometimes pretty awful things that happen to people. For Ben and I, given a choice between blindly accepting Gods omnipotence and deliberately focusing on His goodness, we've chosen to settle for the latter.

Perhaps unfairly, we had attributed much of Ben's breakdown to his life-long experience of evangelical Christianity. It is true that both his breakdown and alcohol addiction stemmed in no small part from his inability to see himself as a person of intrinsic value and worth. Ben's long-held concept of God as an arbitrary, overbearing, critical patriarch who both loved him enough to die for him and hated him enough to condemn him to hell twisted his head up in ways I can't even describe. In the end, and it almost was *the end*, nothing that Ben could pray or reason or read or hear or think or believe could redeem him. Only the sacrificial love Ben received in the Christian rehab was able to reach him and indeed, save his life. You can read more about this and the power of sacrificial love to transform lives in the chapter *Jesus Lives In A Rehab – Who Knew?*

Despite all the good stuff that's happened since Ben came back home, I still suffer from the pesky anxiety disorder, and the panic attacks that come with it. Naturally, I would rather not, but as anyone who experiences them knows, you don't choose them. No moron would choose them. They are not fun, and they are the exact opposite of attention seeking. When you're having one, attention is the last thing you want. Come near me when I'm having one, and I might even punch you in the head. Besides, panic attacks don't attract the kind of attention you might expect. People don't fawn over you and say, "Whatever is the matter, dear?" No, they do not. They walk quickly away dragging their loved ones and belongings with them. It's something about the perspiring and the babbling, and the pupils like pinpricks.

But back to the book.

God, Please Take My Mental Illness is a collection of essays and blog posts on various topics I've written over the last year or so. Many have been previously published online either on my own blog[*], or on other sites such as Burnside Writers Collective[†], Mamamia[‡] or BlogHer[§]. I've edited most, changed a few, and even combined several that have previously appeared as a series. I've arranged them chronologically, as they appeared on my blog. If you'd like to leave me feedback, or send me your comments on any of these, please email me at mail@johilder.com or visit my blog at http://www.johilder.com and leave a comment on the Contact Me page.

I'd also like to let you know that I have another book in the works. *Things Not To Say To Someone Who Has Cancer* tells the story of my experiences while being diagnosed and treated for cancer. Hopefully, *Things Not To Say* will be published sometime in 2012/2013.

---

[*] Jo Hilder – Writer. My website and blog. http://www.johilder.com

[†] Burnside Writers Collective is a US based online magazine for Christians looking for a connection with the world outside of franchise Christianity. http://burnsidewriters.com

[‡] Mamamia is an Australian and international current affairs and commentary, founded by publisher and former magazine editor, Mia Freedman. http://www.mamamia.com.au

[§] The BlogHer website is devoted to creating online opportunities for more than 34 million women who blog. http://www.blogher.com

Any mental health professional will tell you that mental illness and religion really do have a lot in common. Lots of people, in fact – many of them my relatives - think they are probably the exact same thing. Maybe they're right. But before you read the rest of these essays, here's five things I've learned which I think apply to both Christianity and mental illness. -

1) There are some basic principles that apply that simply can't be changed, so don't try and change them or it will make you crazy. *Crazier.*

2) There is also a fair amount of stuff open to discussion, and your voice is as valid as anyone else's, so don't let anyone tell you otherwise.

3) When people tell you "this is the way we do things here", just remember you always have a choice.

4) If it changed you, it will change others too. Your story matters.

5) When in doubt, love is the answer.

All things considered, I'd be deliriously happy if God would take all the mental illness away from my life. Apart from the fact I've had quite enough drama up to this point, it sure would make mixing in large crowds far less embarrassing. But I've had to consider the downside. If being freed from a mental illness means also taking away my ability to hear God when He speaks to me, and I really do believe He speaks to me, then things can stay just as they are, thank you very much.

Enjoy. ☺

1

I'll Love You When You're More Like Me

I bought this great T-shirt last month, at an op-shop, practically brand new, and it's already my absolute favourite. It's emerald green, with a slogan printed in white across the chest. I just love wearing this freaking shirt, however, I think I've worked out why the previous owner was keen to get rid of it. Everywhere I go, people read it and their smile just crumbles away. Questioning eyes meet mine. I can tell they're thinking, "Er, that shirt is a joke, right?"

It reads, "I'll love you when you're more like me."

I have a theory about people's reactions to my shirt - they're either thinking, "That's funny, because I know someone who thinks like that", or else they're thinking, "Is that supposed to be funny? *Because I think like that*."

I like my T-shirt, because it's fun to pretend no one would ever be so unkind as to expect others to change to earn their love. But this thing of expecting someone to change to earn our approval happens so much we have names for it. Names like abuse. Peer pressure. Emotional blackmail. Sometimes, we even call it church.

You know how it goes. *You are just so great. You're awesome, in fact. I think you're terrific. Now, change. Let's just get you all fixed up. This is the way we do things here. Let me show you - no, not that way – this way. There, that's better. Now we can be friends, family, community. I am yours, and you are mine, and you are one of us. You belong.*

For a lot of people, fixing others up is just part of loving them properly, and we've told people this is what God is all about too. God loves you so much He wants to change you. He wants to make you all better. He wants to bless you. God wants to transform your life, and make it into a life worth living. As opposed to the one you have now. But one big problem with telling people God loves them and just can't wait to change them is that you risk convincing them they are broken, sick and poor when perhaps they're really not. Another problem is that when people believe they are fundamentally less-than at their most basic level because everyone keeps telling them they need to be changed all the time, they end up believing they can never be fixed-up enough.

A very wise lady once told me "we all need love the most when we deserve it the least". But instead of giving people our unconditional positive regard and then just letting God do what God does, we Christians have learned to give people just enough love to hook them in, before informing them that to get the rest of it, they'll need to undergo our comprehensive self-improvement program.

Christians have always believed in the idea of salvation, but I think we stopped understanding what we need salvation from long ago. Most people in our society have more than enough of just about everything, and thus have plenty of ways to avoid the desperate measures that can drive people to desperate measures to get their needs met. When Jesus Christ was here with skin on, we find Him interacting with the very poor, the very hungry, the very oppressed and the very marginalized – in fact, he was dealing with the real and pressing social problems of His day. But today, most people we know are already blessed with jobs, houses and good health, so Christians had to make up new ways to be poor, broken and inadequate, just so Jesus has something to save us from. Cured from our poverty, most of our diseases and a vast majority of our social inequalities, Christians have started a new campaign - intense micro-management of everybody's intrinsic character flaws. Rather than making us generous to a flaw, our blessedness and hyper-comfort has made us hypercritical, and not just of ourselves.

God loves you. And I love you. At least I will. When God is all done with you.

There are an awful lot of people walking around who believe in God, but who don't think He loves them very much. And they hear other Christians about all the changes He wants to make to their character and their circumstances, and they just feel very, very tired. When it comes to God's love, I fear we've reinvented it into a kind of hamster wheel of expediential personal development and behavior modification. Once you start running on that wheel, you have no way of ever knowing if you're ever actually getting anywhere, or if it will ever end.

What if it was a Christian's job simply to tell people the Good News of the gospel of Jesus Christ, and tell them God loves them? *Hey friend, have you met Jesus? Jesus – my friend, friend – Jesus. Now I'll just leave you two to get acquainted.* What if it's not actually our job as Christians to diagnose, imagine, organize or facilitate the change we want to see in others? Not by any means? Especially when it means withholding our love, approval and friendship?

What if God doesn't actually feel about everyone the way we feel about ourselves?

Christians must stop this infernal making people over in our own image, firstly because it's the pinnacle of arrogance, and secondly because in doing so, we are effectively saying *God will love all of you more when you're more like us.*

*****

The apostle Paul wrote the Ephesians a letter[**], and as he was wont to do, he began it with a loving greeting. He writes to these early Christians in the spirit of reconciliation between the Jews and Gentiles that were among them, a prayerful encouragement of how they ought to pray for and think of others in the early church.

Paul writes –

"I have not stopped giving thanks for you, remembering you in my prayers."

Paul says to the Ephesians, rather than thanking God that you're not like those other people, give thanks for them. Be grateful for your community, your diversity, your family and your circle of fellowship, whoever they may be. Thank God you are liked, and have folks who like you. Then pray and care for the ones God has placed in your circle of influence and

---

[**] Ephesians 1:16 - 19

concern. Pray for them, because you care for them, and they care for you. All are interdependent.

"I keep asking that the God of our Lord Jesus Christ, the glorious Father, may give you the Spirit of wisdom and revelation, so that you may know him better."

Ask God - that is, *pray* - that He may unfasten the hearts of your friends and family so they *may* (no obligation) look out from their world and see Him everywhere. Pray that they *may* (not must) recognize the Spirit that blazes truth, teaches wisdom and reveals Himself, without guile, agenda and partiality, in other words, who is *nothing like you*. And all this for the sole purpose of getting to know God better, perhaps even before we have had a chance to change anything about ourselves, or about someone else, according to our preferences and our prejudices.

"I pray also that the eyes of your heart may be enlightened..."

Paul says to earnestly desire that the people you commune with *may* (not necessarily) begin to open their hearts to you and to God – not because you see them as a potential project for God to work on, but because *they have seen the real you* – the real, authentic you, exposed, vulnerable and unafraid to show who you really are. A heart is enlightened when the burden of having to change to be accepted and loved for someone else is lifted

"…in order that you may know the hope to which he has called you…"

He, our Father, calls us all to hope. Hope that we can be a part of His Story – the great love story that began at Creation and leads us like any good story - with twists and turns – onward through time toward a passionate reconciliation. There is no *all fixed up*, no need for forced perfection, no projects or makeovers or manhandling – just us saved sinners – for everyone, a level playing field.

"….the riches of his glorious inheritance, and his incomparably great power for us who believe."

So we, the ones who believe, are given this *incomparably great power* as a gift from God, never to be used for exercising superiority, judgment or oppression, but given to empower us to do what God asks of us. In essence, it's *grace* that he gives us. As recipients of this glorious inheritance, we may never, ever presume entitlement. God's grace indeed never qualifies us for anything other than to have Christ's glorious righteousness draped around our shoulders, and His love lavished upon our person.

Real change never comes when it is demanded. Whilst we have the *power* to demand and even to enforce change in others, we never have the right. When that power to enforce change is surrendered, strangely enough, the best conditions for change to occur are created. And this is what God always does in His dealings with us.

So, thusly robed in the free gift of God's grace, and being as we are unable to actually do anything apart from it, how can we ever look at anyone again as merely a potential candidate for change, even in God's name? Jesus basically hung out a shingle which read "Come to me, all you who have had enough of the heavy burdens of men, because I give you a rest from all that.††"

––––––––––––––––––––

†† Matthew 11:28

2

The Illuminati Of The Peri-Menopausal

I've just read in the Sunday paper about this "new" phenomenon of the female mid-life crisis. Apparently, up until quite recently, middle-aged women didn't actually have crises. Try telling that to past generations of women who had only Valium or insanity to retreat to when their husbands took up "working late" and heading off for "weekend conferences interstate". If you ask me, the only precursor I know of for many of the crises women suffer from is having ever known or lived with men. But I digress.

There is something that happens to women when they leave their late thirties. It's not so much a crisis, however, as it is a revelation. Unlike many men, women don't wake up at the age of forty and wonder why the world doesn't understand and appreciate them - they wake up and realise they don't understand and appreciate themselves.

From the ages of about eighteen to thirty-eight, most women believe they will never be as good as everyone else in the world, including other women. We spend our teenage years unable to see our own inherent beauty and vitality. We try all through our twenties to be sexy as our duty to men, and at the same time smart and successful as our duty to our liberationist forebears. We enter our thirties believing that by this age, we should have the perfect body, children, husband, home and career because for crying out loud, we have been at it for about fifteen years and we should have gotten it right by now. Told in our childhoods we had the right never to be violated, oppressed or abused by anyone, by our late thirties we sadly discover most of us have been anyway. Then we reach our forties. Our husbands leave us, our children rebel against us, and our bodies betray us. The "all" we are supposed to have is divided up in court settlements, sent to family counseling and lopped off along with a course of chemotherapy.

In middle-age, many women realise they have expected too much from themselves. By this time we absolutely *know* that we can't have everything. We have come to realise that what we have now will probably be what we have when we're sixty, except it may all be closer to the ground. We've also learned that we can't be all things to everyone else, so we stop trying. Most of us have had at least one health scare, or at least lost someone very close to us. Forced to change our view of life, we now accept we are not immortal or bulletproof. We know we're not young any more, but we also know we're not old…just yet. Middle-aged women don't generally rush out and buy sports cars and get young lovers, although some do. More often, we simply take a look at what we do have, and decide to make the most of it in whatever time we think we have left.

Some decide that what they have at forty is a body they have kept cellulite-free and size double D for twenty years, and venture out to see how much trouble it can get them into. Others decide the reasons they didn't write or paint or travel or study when they were younger no longer exist, i.e.: they no longer believe they are dull, stupid and responsible for the happiness of others, so they take the limitations off themselves and go for it. A woman's mid-life realisations often are more of a crisis to others around them than they are to themselves. Some middle-aged women come to accept that they possibly only have a few years left with the capacity for cognitive and intelligent conversation, so they decide to leave their monosyllabic house-mate in his recliner with a TV dinner, and head off to a book club or lecture theatre instead. One could see how this might cause problems.

Unlike most men, women often have less to lose anyway. Middle-aged women are less likely to see their assets as an extension of their egos, because this generation of women are accustomed to earning less, and sacrificing what they do have for their families. Middle-aged women will fight as hard to keep her family together, seeing that as part of her identity, as a man might exert in leaving it to prove his.

Middle-aged women have been largely invisible in our society. It's taken a re-emergence of us as a force - albeit in tattoo parlours and universities - for that society to even acknowledge we do exist. And then, they have the hide to dismiss us as menopausal shrews; as nothing more than the demographic responsible for the unhappiness of a whole generation of brilliant, misunderstood and apparently incredibly good-looking middle-aged men. May I point out that even the most successful Self-Made Man came out of a woman's body at some point?

This female mid-life crisis thing they are trying to label us with is a ruse, a myth and a lie. There is something going on, but I can tell you, it's no crisis - it's more of an *enlightenment*. As for me, yes, I've had my nose pierced and got myself three large tattoos since I turned forty. Yes, I've dreadlocked my hair and bought skinny jeans – in a size 14. Yes, I went roller-skating last Sunday and I refuse to wear Cottontails. But let me tell you, if you don't like the look of my cellulite, you're standing way too close to my butt. Just hand over the pink slip to your V8 pal, and no one gets hurt.

3

From Burial to Banqueting Table

A while ago, a man I considered to be quite wise at the time said to me
"People change, but not that much." I didn't know quite what to make of
his comment, probably because the person who said it was actually our
pastor. I've always believed a pastors' job is to help people who want to
change, and that believing someone is capable of doing the thing you're
employed to help them with would be a pre-requisite to holding the job.
Apparently not. Maybe he was a bit jaded. Maybe it was time for a new
job. In any case, I didn't believe him. I think people can change, in fact, I
know they can. Maybe we need to invite our old pastor around to our place
house for dinner one of these days. He needs to see what God has done at
my house.

Last Tuesday night, my husband Ben and I had guests for dinner. Fourteen
people sat around our table and ate my lamb roast, including the two of us.
A minor miracle occurred that night, but I think only I, and perhaps our
children, really noticed it. What happened was that Ben was present for the
meal *the whole time.* Of course, you'd have to know what it was like
before to understand how this is different. We didn't invite folks over to

our house for dinner. There was no point. If people came to visit, Ben would say hello, then remain present for about one minute and forty-five seconds after that before disappearing. I don't know how he managed to convince himself that nobody notices when the host goes MIA, but then I'm not sure he ever considered the possibility that his absences were conspicuous to others. The fact is, regardless of if we had two people over, or twenty, Ben would always be a no show at his own dinner party.

After last Tuesday evenings dinner, as we were getting ready for bed, Ben congratulated me for cooking a roast dinner for so many people. "That was a real success, wasn't it?" I froze in the middle of putting on my pyjama pants. Huh? Since when did my husband consider us socialising something he could *succeed* at? Success once involved Ben remaining absent from company without appearing to have had a very quiet but crippling accident in another part of the house. Success was measured by the number of beers he could smuggle out of the house and gulp down before I found him crouched behind some bushes in the back yard. Success was when Ben managed to reappear – either sober, or at all, I wasn't fussy - after leaving very early in the proceedings just to *visit the bathroom*. And this very same person today thinks a dozen people cramped around our dining table eating our food for three hours constitutes a *success*? Just who are you, and what have you done with my husband?

You see, as far as social situations were concerned, Ben was a supreme master of the duck and weave. His avoidance of people and acute need to be alone was different from those occasions where he was simply busy, like in the shed fixing something, washing the car or going for a walk to get the newspapers. Our family had a pet name for it– skulking. *Where's dad? Skulking. Oh.* I think the way Ben saw it, he was only out of the room for a few minutes. The problem was that he was only out of the room for a few minutes, twenty or more times a day - for about twenty years.

It was not much better if we went to other people's houses. On arrival, Ben would spend a few minutes casing the joint, and a few moments later he'd be gone. For years, a lot of people at our church didn't know I was actually married. Someone even asked me out on a date, and I had to tactfully explain I was in fact not a single mother.

When Ben was skulking, he wasn't just out of the room, on a special mission, or even busy. He wasn't writing a thesis or building an ark in the back yard. He was *hiding*. From us. From everyone. And it hurt. When the person you're married to can't hang out with his wife and his kids and your friends and both your parents for any length of time without having to leave and be alone for a while, it's difficult not to be offended. For a long time I thought it was my fault. Ben's anti-social behaviour confirmed my own deep suspicion that I was just *too much*. I came to the sad conclusion my personality was so overwhelming that it made other people unable to function normally in society anymore. So I did what many women do when they blame themselves for their husbands' faults - I covered for him. And when that grew tiresome - because explaining to guests that your husband has something *very important* to do out in the back yard while you are all sitting in his living room does grow tiresome - I just stopped inviting people over anymore.

While the hiding was a problem, it was never *the* problem, and while it wasn't me that broke Ben, Ben was broken just the same. I understand now that when people are broken like Ben was and they feel they ought to be able to fix what's wrong and put it all right but they just can't, they do whatever it takes to feel safe. Often, they do what Ben did and they hide, in all kinds of places, and use all kinds of things to hide behind. Some people don't physically hide like Ben did, but they are hiding all right. They hide behind their work, their possessions and positions, their success, and they even hide behind failure.

There was a story in our local paper this week of an elderly man who died when his house burnt down during the night with him inside it. Neighbours said he was an eccentric recluse who shut himself away in the 1960's when his wife left him after only a few months of marriage. A bricklayer, he had built the house himself before their wedding. Firefighters said his home was crammed with newspapers, photographs and all kind of rubbish, the result of decades of hoarding. They said if it were not for the stuff in his house, he might have escaped the fire. He died as he'd lived, safe in his well-built house, surrounded by his history, safe from judgment and failure.

Far better men than Ben have been hiders. Adam, the very first man on the planet, was a hider.‡‡ As skulkers go, in my opinion, Adam wasn't particularly good at it. I can say this because I've lived with a real pro. Adam gave in way too early for starters - he was only in those bushes for ten minutes, tops. I hate to brag, but Ben had far more stamina that that. And what's with Adam taking an accomplice along for the skulk? Pros never take an accomplice. Any crime they committed may be a shared experience, but shame is always a solo venture. I suspect Adam was really only playing possum – I think Adam kind of wanted to be found.

While long-term hiding requires a lot of staying power, it can get kind of boring. While Ben was hiding, he found that smoking cigarettes and drinking alcohol really helped to keep his hands busy. These also conveniently helped him to forget exactly how many hours a day he was actually spending skulking. I had my suspicions Ben skulked at work too,

---

‡‡ Genesis 3:8 – 10

because whenever I rang to talk to him, nobody could ever find him. But I think it was the day I opened up some boxes under the house and hundreds of empty beer bottles fell out I realised I might have underestimated exactly how much of his life both his skulking, and the habits that kept him occupied while he was doing it, were consuming.

I didn't understand for a long time exactly what Ben was so ashamed of, even after I worked out Ben was hiding. Ben is not and never has been a really bad man. He hasn't been in any trouble with the police, or been unfaithful in our marriage. He is a gentle, patient father and has a quiet disposition. Ben's wrongdoings are certainly no worse than any other simple mans, springing as they do from the common natural weaknesses and shortcomings of all human beings. But I've come to understand that shame is not logical. It's not circumstantial. Shame is not even natural. Shame wasn't there at the beginning, when God created people. I mean they walked around without clothes for goodness sake. Shame was *learned*. Shame was a mutation. Shame was human invention, and it filled the place where something else used to be.

Relationship.

I imagine the first garden, its two occupants living in complete intimacy with each other and their creator. So guileless was the communion between the two humans they had nothing but their different skins to separate them. But then they did something they were told not to do by someone that loved them. Afterwards, the first thing they did was to go and make clothes to put on top of their skin. *Don't look at me.* Then, forgetting He had always been able to see them, they realised that not only could they be seen by each other, the creator could see them too. When they heard the creator coming, they hid behind some bushes. *What's happened to us?* they asked themselves, *we never worried about being seen before?* The thing is, when the creator found out what they did, He didn't demand they take off their clothes again, in fact, he turned around and made them both some better ones.

Ben – my sweet, gentle Ben - was not a bad person, but something inside him didn't want to be seen. He thinks it started when he was very young. Ben was a quiet, covert and sneaky child, secretly setting fires to things and learning to hide stolen treasures from his parents. For the longest time Ben believed that God was a violent, iron-fisted Father, quick to anger and slow to forgive, particularly a very naughty boy like he was. After many years of just trying to stay out of God's way, he found a way to hide that worked, and after a while he forgot what it was ever like to walk in the light.

When I became ill with cancer in 2003, Ben was already spiritually and emotionally unstable. The issues that my illness raised in our relationship and in our faith challenged him in the deepest parts of his being. He floundered with feelings of helplessness and depression, without any way to draw on the grace, strength and comfort from God or me he so desperately needed. He thought God was up there waggling his head, telling him to harden up and get a backbone. Ashamed of his inability to protect his family from harm, and from the consequences of his weakness in its aftermath, he pulled even further inside himself. If God had come calling "where are you?" Ben couldn't have heard Him, because he was ensconced under the house with a cigarette and a six-pack of beer, medicating his despair.

After a few more years, things really fell to pieces. He lost his business, leaving us tens of thousands of dollars in debt. We had to leave town so Ben could get a new job. He became more disenfranchised from his children, the elder three of whom were now in their teens. Our resentment for each other grew and festered between us like a tumour. The last skerrick of Bens' belief in himself disintegrated the same time as his desire to stay married to me. Desperate to save his life, I sent Ben away. By now, I was the only one of us with enough self-esteem left to survive being seen as the bad guy that broke up our marriage. Thank God, at that time a place in a Christian rehabilitation centre came up before Ben totally disintegrated.

In rehab, Ben learned to stay both literally and emotionally in the room with his shame, now compounded by the collapse of our family and the loss of everything he had and had been. All of the structures and devices he had created to keep himself safe were broken and useless. In that place of absolute vulnerability, Ben found his father God running towards him with His arms outstretched.

Finally, my boy, I've found you.

Since then, I have seen my husband rise up from a long sleep of self-hate and humiliation and sit up to God's banqueting table. He is making a right pig of himself, I can tell you. The compassion I see in my husbands' eyes these days, as he tells me about his wish to help the people God brings across his path, makes me fall back in wonder. How God can take a man who emptied himself out in self-disgust and fill him again with such goodness and compassion is beyond my comprehension.

Change is possible, I know it. I've seen shame, fear and guilt stunt a human soul into a crooked shadow of its former self, and then I saw that same human being raised up from the dead. Shame is fruitless, pointless in fact, particularly the shame we inflict upon each other. It's only mercy that brings the withered ones stumbling forth for healing. The enemy wants us bound in the dark, wrapped in the rags of our self-loathing, but God wants us free in the light where He and the entire world can see us for who we really are.

I want to tell you, if you love someone that is dead while they live, don't give up hope. People can change – more than you can even dream of. I thought Ben was gone forever, but I was wrong. He came back. Now I know Ben doesn't like it when I brag about him, but I just can't help myself. I doubt that anyone present for dinner on Tuesday night would have any real idea why I was gazing at Ben in wonder as he carved the lamb and cracked the jokes. There, I thought to myself, thanks to the grace of God, goes my husband, the most amazing man I have ever known.

4

Why It's So Hard To Love Others

I used to think alcoholics lay around on park benches in trench coats with brown paper bags clutched to their wheezing chests. I though they teetered on bar stools until closing time while their wives, vacantly clutching a cigarette and staring at an empty dining chair, explained to the children *daddy's working late again*. I saw all this on TV, so it must be true. Alcoholics were not *us* - they were *others*. That was until my husband became an alcoholic.

My husband didn't frequent bars or park benches. My husband didn't even think he could have been an alcoholic before he went to his first A.A. meeting. There he met people who were not park bench dwellers or bar stool teeterers - they were secretaries, real estate agents and builders with careers, families and mortgages. They were not *others*. They were just like him.

We'd all like to think we are not one of the others, but we are all others to someone. We're all in some ways good and bad, strangers and friends, aliens and natives. And because we all are others, when we judge others, we judge ourselves.

Jesus often said why not love other people the same way we love ourselves, because He understood that when we do this, they stop being others and become *one-anothers*. One-anothers are not the same thing as others. The very word 'other' denotes difference, whilst "one-another" means simply another one of what and who we are. If we can stop seeing everyone else as different from us in some way, and see everyone else as being exactly like us in the ways that count, I think we're getting closer to loving like Jesus suggested we do.

But we don't.

The problem is not that we don't know how to love people - it's that we have this *others* mentality in the first place. Others has come not to mean other people, it has come to mean other sexual preferences, other religions, other genders, other ways of seeing and being which are different from our own. We look around us and see not one hundred people who need love and regard, but one hundred reasons not to love or regard people.

But why do we wait until people change to be more us before we love and regard them? Why wait until they put more on or take more away? Why wait until they walk our way or talk our way?

Jesus didn't say "love others as I have loved you". He said "love **one another** as I have loved you". In Jesus eyes, there were no others, only people, just like himself – *one-anothers*. We see people as *we* are, not as *they* are. When there is a mote in the eye, it makes the seer think the problem is a beam floating out there in space. No wonder the world looks like such a mess.

5

Jesus Lives In A Rehab – Who Knew?

I have been a Christian my whole adult life. I've also ministered in many churches over the years, and I consider that to have been a privilege. I've received via those same churches some very useful information about how to improve myself, and assorted methods of navigating my life with wisdom and propriety. And then last year, my husband, also a Christian his adult life, was admitted to a rehabilitation centre for alcoholism. Our marriage broke up. Our family in tatters, I looked to my Christianity for answers, and to my church for support, and I have to say, I found both a bit thin on the ground. What happened to us *just isn't meant to happen to Christians*. What the hell went wrong?

When I went to visit my husband in rehab for the first time three months into his stay, I encountered something I had never seen before in thirty years of Christianity. I met a bunch of fairly uncharismatic people doing God's work without flash and for the most part, without cash. This was a *ministry*? Where were all the energetic interns, the slick banners, the stacks of audio-visual equipment and the glossy brochures? When I pulled into the muddy driveway and wandered down to the communal eating area beside the converted railway carriages, I found I couldn't tell the rehab inmates (or *seekers*) from the staff. Everyone looked exactly the same. When someone came up to me to shake my hand, I wasn't sure if the guy was a reforming addict or the manager.

Um, I'm looking for the – er- staff? I was thinking to myself, w*here exactly are all the Christians?*

It took me a few weeks of visiting to work out how the place operated, and why it was so different from any other Christian organisation I'd ever some across. Sherwood Cliffs is made up of Christian families, volunteers and seekers blended into a small, interdependent community. Everyone works either on the farm, milking cows, growing food or on building and maintenance, or in the kitchen or the school. Everyone gets together to share a meal at least once a day, sometimes more. Everyone attends regular Christian devotions, and everyone gets on the bus and goes to church on Sundays. But even though these guys called themselves a Christian community, something about it all made me feel very, very uneasy. Here was a bunch of Christians all in one place, but there was no pastor writing sermons in a corner office, no music director and no coffee machine. Was this some kind of cult? Where was the structure I was accustomed to, the one every bunch of Christians I'd ever met just seemed to naturally organize itself into? Where did the leadership team hierarchy begin and end? Why didn't these people get themselves properly organized? It was all so confusing. I'd never had any trouble working out where I fit in with Christians before. I've got my worship leader badge, I'm a card carrying, Titus-2-type, *older woman*, I even have a Bible College qualification. Excuse me, but exactly what kind of a Christian gig are you guys running here? I have no idea where I'm supposed to fit. Don't you people know who I am?

Sure, you're the wife of that alcoholic guy over there. Would you like a sausage sandwich?

Nobody important here, sweetheart, just us saved sinners.

Until I grew a little more accustomed, it shocked me that anyone believed they could run a successful ministry that way. The rehab staff – all volunteers - weren't trying to find ways to solicit money, to get people to join their church, or even trying to get people *saved*. They just lived a simple, devotional life alongside one other, working through issues as they came up, hour-by-hour, day-by-day. The ones who had faith in Christ lived Christ, and those simple words and actions, along with the fact they did what they did from an attitude of servitude and compassion, spoke Gods love in buckets. No preaching, no guilt or shame, no pressure and no fuss. Just milking cows together, praying together, eating together and digging ditches together.

People living with Jesus, and Jesus living with the people.

Sometimes the seekers wanted more of what they saw and heard in the Christians, but sometimes they just said, "thanks very much" and left. My husband, a born-again Christian his entire life, initially resisted the program, citing his observation that "I'm not like these people - I'm a *Christian*". Eventually, Ben came to accept that eve though he was a Christian when he came here, he was nothing special – just another hopeless alcoholic who had lost everything he ever held dear who really needed help. Ben and I had an opportunity to see Jesus Christ lived – not just talked about - by real men in a tangible way every day as everyone went about the business of life. This wasn't just the theory of Jesus – this was the reality. Now, Ben argued. He hid himself. He bargained and complained and justified himself. But Jesus won. After three months, we reconciled our marriage while he was still in rehab. After completing six months, Ben came back to us, whole and healed.

Now Ben is home again, we've kept our ties with this amazing place. It's where after all those years of being Christians, we found Jesus, and became his disciples.

We've come to learn that a disciple is more than just a follower or a fan.

48

It's more than just someone who knows the program and knows how to work it. A disciple isn't just someone who does Christianity, vocationally or even devotionally. Jesus had crowds of people following him around, talking about what he did and said and even being transformed by his words and deeds, but they were not his disciples. They were certainly his fans and followers, perhaps even his stalkers, but they were not the ones He chose to really follow Him. A disciple is immersed in the teachings of the master, following in his steps, living the lifestyle and applying the practices spiritually and practically, even when nobody sees or knows. Quietly. Simply. Sacrificially. In fact, I truly believe it was the sacrificial love demonstrated by those volunteers in rehab that finally broke through Ben's addiction. When he arrived at the realization that those walking beside him, caring for him and supporting him had laid down their lives to do it, knowing full well he'd done nothing to deserve it, it changed everything.

I think we as Christians have been very much focused on eliminating sins through behavior modification, on making good citizens, on training effective leaders, passionate speakers and savvy financiers and not been particularly interested in making genuine Disciples of Christ. I think we need to get back to the table and have a look at what on earth we are doing about the latter, and forget about most of the former. *Because it isn't working.* And when I say working, I don't mean as in producing perfect, fixed-up people. I mean it's not working in saving people from addictions, from marriage breakdowns, from depression, or even from their own pride. In speaking with the workers at the rehab, I heard time and time again, "Give me ten un-churched addicts to work with over one guy who comes here already a Christian. They know all the scriptures and have all the answers. But we tell them, 'buddy, you may know it all, but you're still in rehab just like that other guy.'"

I see now that there are major differences between the Christianity I learned, and the practice of Christian discipleship that brings about the real changes in people that sometimes saves their lives.

Number one, it's not about dynamic leadership.

Compared to some of today's contemporary church leaders, particularly the ones with huge public profiles, Jesus was a fairly hopeless leader. Instead of being energised by crowds, he scarpered off quite a lot whenever big groups gathered. He showed little interest in important people whom might have gained him favour with authorities. Instead, Jesus hung out with low-lifes, eating in their houses and allowing himself to be pawed by them. He would not govern as Moses had, nor did he throw his weight around. When people asked him to judge their trivial differences, he spoke about the bigger, eternal picture, and they grew frustrated with his convoluted language. The Jews had expected an apocalyptic Messiah, who would come to depose the Romans and lead Israel to freedom. The Bible speaks of Jesus as having nothing particularly charismatic about him – he just got on with his work. Jesus first disciples were tradesmen, never having progressed from the primary school of the Torah to Jewish Bible College. Discipleship, it seems, requires only a willingness to learn from Christ's life and teachings. Any fisherman can do it.

Number two - it's also not about being well-behaved, compliant or passive.

Jesus was not meek and mild. The way he spoke was often obnoxious and argumentative, particularly when addressing the leaders and teachers of his day. He shouted a lot, and was quite combative. Violating customs, he talked openly to women in public, and allowed prostitutes to touch his body. He made a whip and used it in church, on people. He once addressed his closest friend by accusing him of being directed by Satan. Jesus was not "nice."

Three - it's not about money.

Jesus didn't give anyone money, and he didn't take anyone's money. He paid taxes, but didn't work for a living. Jesus didn't give advice on money except to say that having a lot of it would make it difficult to do God's work, and heaping it up in one place was selfish. Jesus spoke about attitudes and intentions concerning money, and nothing about the vast accumulation or multiplication of it. As far as Jesus was concerned, true treasures were not of this earth.

Four - it's not about being a "winner" in life.

Jesus did exactly what God told him to do from beginning to end. He told people where he had come from, explaining his mission the whole time. People knew he had been a carpenter, and who his parents were; he was not some blow-in, snake oil salesman. He obeyed God explicitly the whole of his public life. However, the very people he was sent to help murdered him. He served then he died, without ever becoming the successful public figure others hoped he might. In terms of his lifetime achievements and his public profile, Jesus was not a winner.

When my husband and I first encountered the true person and character of Jesus Christ in Christians, we simply didn't recognize it, even after a lifetime of what we knew as Christianity. In rehab, we found Jesus wasn't actually a system to be negotiated, a technique to be applied or a society to be starred in. In fact, Jesus was only ever and exactly what He always claimed to be. Our salvation. When we found Jesus, we got saved from everything that had us bound in the dark and all the other toxic crap we'd become addicted to - including our particular brand of Christianity.

Jesus Christ is not merely a method, but is *the way*. Jesus is our *true north,* the direction His disciple always needs to be headed in. Christ is not merely the facts - not just a historical figure to be studied and categorized and referenced - but is *the truth*. To live Christ is to espouse the essence of what really is right now, not always what we wish life was like or choose to pretend it is. Living truthfully in the moment allows us to release our pride and our pretense and fall back into the arms of grace. Jesus Christ is not just a lifestyle, but is *the life* – the beginning, the journey, and the end of all things. When it comes to the gospel, He is not merely a pointer. Jesus Christ is the whole point.

Jesus lives in a rehab – who knew? That's where we met Him for the very first time. The work of the volunteers at Sherwood Cliffs Christian Community continues. To be a part of this ministry, please visit the website: http://www.sherwoodcliffs.com.au/ Or you can support their work by making a donation via Paypal on my website. http://www.johilder.com

6

Raising Awareness Of The Issues Raised

By Raising Breast Cancer Awareness

I'd like to share with you a conversation I have quite often, which usually begins when someone "Did you hear such-and-such has cancer?"

I might say something like "Yes, I heard. Did you know I had cancer?"

"Oh, are you okay now? Did you have treatment?"

"Chemotherapy and radiotherapy."

"Wow, that's intense." And then follows the inevitable. "And which breast was it in? Did you have a mastectomy? Do you have - like – *a fake one*?"

Now, I know I brought the subject up first. But apart from the problem with it being perfectly okay to talk about my breasts in general conversation, there's also another issue here. Why is it that everyone assumes, because I am a woman, the only cancer I could have had is *breast cancer*?

Before I go any further, I'd like to give well-deserved kudos of heroic proportions to everyone who has been diagnosed with breast cancer, plus the millions of people who've campaigned to raise money for and increase awareness of the disease worldwide. God knows, all this has to happen. Breast cancer is an insidious, sometimes disfiguring, always terrifying cancer - a horrific disease that, thankfully, we are curing more often every day, due to billions of dollars raised for research, and improving early screening and detection programs. The lives of breast cancer patients are also not just being saved, but also salvaged, thanks to a deeper understanding of the psycho-social effects of breast cancer on patients, and on carers and the wider community.

But while there are certainly positive effects flowing from increased awareness of breast cancer, there are other issues that have arisen as a result - issues which indicate to me, as both a cancer survivor and as someone who works with cancer patients, that people are in danger of making some general, and quite dangerous, assumptions about breast cancer, and also about the people who get it.

Marketing is about brand association, and the brand for breast cancer is the colour *pink*. Long associated with childishness and feminine innocence, pink has been universally substituted for any actual physical images of breast cancer. Everywhere we go we see pink ribbons, pink t-shirts, pink logos and pink bandannas used to sell everything from bottled water to lipstick. There are two problems associated with this broad association of the colour pink with breast cancer. Firstly, not all women who get breast cancer identify with pink, or with the submissive, baby-like femininity it represents. And secondly, not all people who get breast cancer are actually female. Some of them, more than you probably think, are men, and this breast-cancer-always-equals-pink obsession drives them absolutely crazy.

My friend Gary, who comes to my cancer support group, has something like this conversation almost every day.

"Hey Gary, did you hear Frank has cancer?"

"I heard that. Did you know I had cancer?"

"No way, really? What kind of cancer was it? Prostate? Bowel?"

"Actually, I had breast cancer."

Incredulous stare, awkward silence. Men get *breast cancer*? Well, yes, they most certainly do. And Gary has nowhere to go with that in practically every sense - nowhere in conversation, nowhere in people's perceptions, and certainly nowhere in terms of supportive care and services for his particular kind of cancer. Gary has been lobbying the local breast cancer support group in his area to allow men to join in their meetings, and believes they only allowed him to come along in the end when they realized the legal implications of excluding him. Gary has decided he actually feels more comfortable in our group, because we are not cancer or gender specific and we do not exclude carers and partners of cancer patients. Yes, there is such a thing as cancer snobbery, believe me. For Gary, what is of most concern is the widely held assumption is that only women get breast cancer, when the reality is that men (even those *without* man-boobs) can get it too. He has no idea how community attitudes can be changed, when so much work has been done to create an image of breast cancer as a female disease. And before you ask, blue is already taken – for prostate cancer.

Another issue I encounter is the dangerous assumption that breast cancer is the only cancer women need be concerned about. It isn't. Statistics indicate that many cancers previously associated predominantly with men, such as bowel and lung cancer, are killing increasingly more women. I also wonder if other cancers are perhaps considered less disfiguring by women than breast cancer is, if perhaps we fear having our breasts removed more than we do having a lump of skin scooped out, or a section of bowel or a lung taken. The fact is that the physical and lifestyle implications of these other cancers can be equal to or even outweigh those of breast cancer. How many women check their breasts religiously, but continue to smoke cigarettes? Many women fear that giving up smoking will increase their appetites and make them fat. I know a woman who had mouth cancer during the last few months of her life, and while she certainly kept her trim figure, it was mainly because she could no longer eat solid food through the rotting crevasse that was her mouth. The sad fact is that most breast cancer caught early enough can be treated and even cured, but by the time many other cancers are detected it is too late.

Breast cancer is certainly not the only cancer that women need to be aware of. In 2003, at the age of thirty five, I was diagnosed with stage 3B (there are only four stages, and B means it had begun metastasizing) Non-Hodgkin's Lymphoma, and even my family doctor was unconvinced prior to my diagnosis there was anything wrong with me…until I presented to the emergency department of my local hospital on the verge of collapse. I had no obvious lumps or bumps – a perfectly healthy pair of C-cups. Pity about the tumour the size of a saucer buried three centimetres under my sternum, but no one thought to check in there.

I have a friend who, like me, was diagnosed a few years ago with cancer in its later stages. However, unlike me, she can't talk about her diagnosis in general conversation, because no one wants to talk about *vulval* cancer. She didn't even know there was such a thing, yet gynecological cancers like hers, and blood cancers like mine, are not considered statistically to be rare amongst women. Perhaps not rare, perhaps just unheard of – quite literally.

Increased awareness of breast cancer is a double-edged sword. It seems the very changes in perception and awareness that save lives every day may be creating a set of assumptions perhaps as dangerous as our ignorance ever was. I would like to advocate another kind of awareness. Please consider that not everyone diagnosed with breast cancer is female. Many breast cancer patients are men and will never be acknowledged, supported, celebrated or lauded the way many female breast cancer patients and survivors are. They are also more likely to be isolated from appropriate services, marginalised by stigma, and sometimes even ridiculed because of their disease. Also, when you pin on a pink ribbon and forward one of those chain emails, I would like you to remember that not all the cancers women are diagnosed with are breast cancers. Check your boobies by all means, but check your moles, and your motions too. Check your rashes, your rude bits, your lumps and your bumps, wherever they may be. The other side of breast cancer awareness is realizing the scope and the effect *all* kinds of cancer have on every diagnosed person's family and friends, and on the community and society as a whole.

Now *that's* what I call cancer awareness.

7

It's Not About Quality; It's About Permission -

Recovering Our Creativity

"All children are born artists; the trick is to remain one as you grow up." –
Pablo Picasso

My most memorable creative moment happened when I was a small child
of about five or six. It was a significant point in my life as an artist, but
unfortunately, it's all been pretty much downhill from there. I was the kind
of precocious youngster that liked to make sure everyone knew I was
around. I liked to sing and dance and make up plays where I would parade
around in my mother's nightdresses, pretending to be Indian royalty. You
get the picture. I didn't realize that a significant thing was happening in the
actual moment - it's only now when I think back that I really wish I'd held
on to that flash of genius and made it stick with me. If I had, by now I'd
probably have created a vast body of artistic work, but as it stands, I have
wasted about twenty of the last forty-two years not making the art I love so
much. And why? Well, mostly because I was afraid it wouldn't be any
good.

I was singing, you see, just before the memorable moment happened. I was singing my head right off, and by God, I was *good*, just about as good as a five or six year-old can be. I was thinking how amazing it was to be able to produce such a wondrous noise just by opening one's mouth and sending the voice out as big and wide as possible. Now this was not just self-expression or exuberance – this was *technical*. My big 'ole voice could go up and down, and up and down again, and oh, what a *wonderful feeling*! I was quite lost in this place of pure joy, just being a small child singing her heart out, when someone who should have known better interrupted me. "Oh!" they exclaimed, actually putting their hands up over their ears, "What a terrible noise!"

That, by the way, was not the significant moment. It came immediately afterward.

I looked up at the person who should have known better, and I looked them right in their eyes and I thought, you know what? You're *wrong*. You're just wrong, because that was not a terrible noise. That, right there, was some *mighty fine singing*. You don't know *what you're talking about*. And there it was - my most memorable, and probably my finest, artistic moment. I've struggled to get back there ever since.

Oh, if only I'd been able to bring that six year-old back into the room every time I put down my guitar because the inner critic who should have known better said "Oh, what a terrible noise!" I wish all those times I laid down the paintbrush, or pushed my chair away from the keyboard, or dropped out of the dance class, I'd asked that little girl what she thought of me. I wish I'd remembered my significant moment when I burned the romantic poems of my adolescence because I thought they were stupid, and when I refused to play any of my songs in public. I wish I'd run back to her every time my mental perfectionist refused to let me waste time making bad art and made me get a job I was good at instead. Imagine what a musician, what a dancer, what a poet, what a painter, what a writer I'd be by now, if only, if only I'd never stopped every time I heard a voice say "Ah! That's awful! For the love of God, stop it!" I wish that I'd remembered to say "Are you out of your mind? Of *course* it's bad! Who are you – the friggin' *art police*? and then just got on with it anyway.

I know now that it takes a long time to get as good as you'd like to be when you first begin. You learn to do something by doing it, says John Holt, there is no other way. A very wise friend of mine says you need about ten thousand hours to become proficient at something, be it throwing a pot, writing a sonnet, or probably even raising a child. Nobody can make something incredible right away. When it comes to creating art, it's not about quality - it's about permission. And permission to make your art, good, bad and ugly, is a gift only you can give yourself.

Creativity is subversive. It needs room to move. It needs to be allowed to rebel, to think, to explore, to explode, to sleep, to feed and to question. It will eat everything you pop into its mouth and eliminate its waste as its requirements dictate, just like a baby, or an incontinent elderly relative, as the case may be. Your creativity will boldly announce itself as having arrived, and then may sit idly by and do nothing. It may take over, it may even undermine. It may sleep all day, and work all night. But in the end, creativity will be the essence of wonderful, because it is greater than all conventions. If you want to excel in convention, do just what has been done before and merely seek to improve upon it. But if you wish to be an artist, break faith with convention - starve that bastard in the dark, smash it and crush it and put it outside while you fly around the room with paintbrushes and flugelhorns. Chase your convention screaming from the room and throw its pretentious spectacles out after it into the street. Take your creativity and kiss it with passion right on the mouth, then let it kiss you back. Give yourself permission to love that part of you that scares others to death - your muse, your thinker, your child, your dreamer, your explorer, your artist, your heart, your ideas, your creations. They are yours, and that alone makes them great and worthy.

So, get to it. Write that book you cannot find, the one that tells your story.

Sing the song that haunts you in your dreams. Bring your wild vision forth and fill the hungry canvas. Get that art out of you, as if you could push your own heart right out of your mouth. Don't worry about it being wrong, and don't worry about it being good enough. There is no art police but your own inner judge, your critic, your resistance to wrongness and imperfection and mistakes. It's not an awful noise I promise you - it's *wonderful*. Your creativity is not just what you do...it's who you are.

And I...I am the Queen of India.

8

Why Not Reading The Bible

Could Turn Out To Be A Great Idea

I was, and still am, the only individual in my direct family of origin who believes in God – you could say my faith is enigmatic. One night, when I was about four years old, God called me out of bed and drew me to the window of my room, where I really saw for the first time the beauty of a full, white moon and a starry night sky. It was breathtaking, and I still remember it exactly. I heard a voice whisper "Jo, I am here, and all of this is just for you." I knew exactly who it was – it was God. Ever since that night, if I've ever lacked faith, it's only ever been in myself, or perhaps in one or two particularly mercenary teachers at high school. Why do they spend all those years at college to just care so little? But I digress.

As for me and God, I loved our late night mutual admiration society, but I longed to know Him better. I wanted to find out who God really was, and what, if anything, He wanted from me. I started going to church with my best friend. I *luuurrvved* the Mass, because clearly *God was there*. You only had to see the special clothes the priests wore, the gaudy stained-glass windows and the long, wordy songs to know God would be around - I knew he liked the same things I did. However, to my dismay, despite the fact God had spoken to me *personally*, these people wouldn't let me line up for the little white biscuit and the drink in the gold cup. They had special times in church for sitting down and standing up, and important things to say to God at certain intervals that I just couldn't get the hang of. My friend's mum did give me my own set of rosary beads, but she wouldn't teach me the prayer that went with them. I just could never quite make the connections, learn the rules, or it seemed, be a real part of God's on-earth family. I was like God's annoying next-door neighbours kid – the one He only ever talked to over the fence whilst pruning His celestial hedge by the full moon. How did everyone get to know what the rules were? What had God said that made people know this was how you did things? If I was going to be included, clearly I needed inside information. I needed to get my hands on that special book my friends parents had on the dining table. I had to get me a Bible.

One day, a few years later, I stumbled across a hard-cover Gideon's Bible in the drawer of a motel room my family was staying in. I was like Indiana Jones finding an archaeological treasure. I squirreled the thing into my bed and hid with it under the covers, trembling with excitement. At last, now I could learn all the rules! Now I'd know how to make Him happy! I could surprise God at our next meeting by reciting verbatim one of his poems -

ooh, he'd like that. Or maybe even have Him give me a pop quiz! But to my dismay, the Bible made hardly any sense to me. I started at the front, but I'd already heard about Adam and Eve in scripture class. What I needed was the instructions. I skipped to the back. Wow, that was even weirder than the beginning. I tried opening just anywhere, but I came up with lists of such-and-such begat such-and-such. Ugh, boring. I looked up the Jesus bits, which was easy – everything he said was in red. He'd know what to do, being God's actual son and all. But from what I could see, Jesus just seemed to be busy with his friends, going fishing and eating seafood picnics on hillsides, and man, he talked a lot. In frustration, I put the Bible back in the drawer. It seemed like a cruel game. Why God, is it so hard to get to know you?

Years later in my teens, I started going to a charismatic protestant church, and to my relief, they seemed to have an idea of what the Bible was all about. I found out that God says drinking and smoking is bad, and having sex before marriage is a definite no-no. Hmm…perhaps this would be a little harder than I thought. I also learned that God wants us to go out on Friday nights and do street theatre to share the gospel, to let everyone who doesn't come to church know the good news that if they don't get saved like us, they'll burn in hell. Even my exhibitionist self baulked a little. I also found out that the end times were coming and that the bad things that were happening in the world were going to get worse, and that Henry Kissinger was the anti-Christ. That part all turned out to be in that weird section at the end of the Bible. Who knew?

On the brighter side, I also discovered in church that if you're a good Christian and do all the right things by God, you will never have anything bad happen to you, and your life will be long, wonderful and prosperous. Personally, I was so relieved to just finally have a handle on some of the rules, that having God reward me for keeping them was somewhat of a bonus. Still the only God-believing Christian in my family, I just wanted to belong *somewhere*. Finally, perhaps, I would fit into God's family. And, it seemed, I was also going to be fabulously skinny, incredibly wealthy and famous beyond my wildest dreams as well…and all this, in the Bible! Who knew?

But then, over time, something happened. People we knew - God-trusting, Bible-believing people - lost their health, their homes and all their money, sometimes even their faith even though they knew all the rules and read the Bible. Other people died when they weren't supposed to, and people were mean to other people when they didn't need to be. And then, worst of all, despite all my rule-keeping and deep comprehension of the mysteries of the Bible, I got cancer. My husband started drinking. Our family fell apart. We not only didn't get everything we wanted, we got a whole bunch of stuff nobody in their right mind would want. And Our God, the God of the Bible, the God who made up the rules and promised us the world, did nothing to stop it. Eventually, we worked out that either something was wrong with God, or something was wrong with us. We think maybe we've hit on something. It turns out there's nothing wrong with God.

When all the stuff started going down, amongst other drastic things I had to do, I stopped reading the Bible. Not because I thought there was something wrong with it, although clearly it didn't say what I'd always thought it did. I stopped because I suspected there was something wrong with the way I was reading it. Every time I opened my Bible, I was crushed by broken promises. I stumbled over unkeepable rules, and anguished over formulas that hadn't worked to keep us safe and happy. I decided to just leave it alone while I changed into someone else – someone who was prepared to let the word be *The Word*.

It seemed to me that I had been viewing scripture in a mirror of my own wants, needs, hopes and desires. I had flicked past the personally irrelevant parts, as if the immense chronological, cultural and theological significance of the document had no meaning except as it related to my twenty-first century, white, heterosexual, western, middle-class existence. It took a long time to get over my addiction to Biblical fortune telling. I had twenty-something years of church doctrine and practice to undo. Once I began to become hungry again to know who God was, just like I had back in the beginning under the moon and the stars, I wanted to read the Bible again, and it was like I'd never read it at all. It was like fresh, cool water to my parched, thirsty soul.

It's been years since this difficult time. But a couple of weeks ago, after spending six months focused on a very directive Bible study, I decided to set my Bible aside again for a while. I'd begun to read it the way the author of the study wanted me to read it – as supporting evidence for their particular point of view. *I think this – and here's the exact chapter from the Bible parroting what I just said.* The Bible was again becoming less the beautiful, challenging, irrepressible work I know it to be, and more like legal evidence for a prosecution case. That's why I love to read the Message Bible. The absence of those tiny little chapter numbers is the perfect foil for any theologian's carefully organized argument.

And now, after a deliberate Bible fast, I'm getting hungry again. I'll be heading back any minute now, because I'm dry as old bones. I am wracking my brains for those life-giving words, and I'm coming up empty more often than not. The spirit of the Word is slipping away from me and like the lover in Song of Solomon, soon I'll be off in hot pursuit. This is a much better way to live with the Bible, I think. The appetite whet, filled with longing, stumbling off in search of that divine, sweet food - a much better way to be than to reclining petulantly at the table, nibbling away on appetisers, complaining endlessly about your sore toe and your ignorant, charismatic neighbour. When you're jaded, and you think you know it all, when you come to believe you've grown bigger than the Bible, that's perhaps the time when you need to step back a little, until the Bible goes back to being bigger than you, and begins to overwhelm you again. If you've lost your appetite for the Word, fast for a while, and sharpen your hunger for God's way of speaking, for His way of moving, for His way of admonishment, for His way of love. A man whose stomach is full will resist even the sweetness of honey, but to a hungry man, even the bitter is sweet[§§]. Sometimes the Word is harsh and pungent to us, but it always remains the very best of nourishment for the spirit and the soul. Sometimes all you need is an empty stomach.

[§§] Proverbs 27:7

9

Jesus, My Good Friend

I know many of the folks that read my blog aren't big Jesus fans. They all must wonder what on earth I go on and on about sometimes. We go way back, Jesus and I. I suppose I could for the sake of political correctness pretend I don't think he's real or significant, and talk about him in a theological or theoretical way to indicate I'm not a religious nutcase or a member of a cult. But I won't be doing that. Jesus and I made friends when I was very young, and we are still friends despite everything that's happened since we met. I don't blame him for the mistakes I made.

I should point out that he's the one who's been the good friend, not me. I've been relentless in dialogue, but not really a great friend, strictly speaking. I've been pretty hard on him at times - criticizing him for his perceived shortcomings, being annoyed because he wouldn't physically appear in front of me on demand...you know, just the usual friend stuff. I've dragged Jesus into some pretty questionable situations. For instance, I once insisted that he show up to help me not be molested by a trucker my friend and I had invited to stop by the side of the highway via a CB radio. Now three minutes before I was pretty much hoping Jesus was a million miles away.

But the second I saw that trucker walk around the front of my friends VW Beetle and make toward us, I wished Jesus would just pop out from under the hood with a pair of nun-chucks and go to work. Thankfully, we escaped the trucker, and Jesus never had to use his nun-chucks. Soon after that, I learned to use my *commonsense.*

He must have gotten so tired of me in my teenage years. But unlike many others who had to put up with my antics back then, Jesus is still my friend, despite knowing full well just how stupid I can be. And also unlike many others who had to tolerate my wild days, Jesus never ever brings it up in conversation. *Thank God.*

But despite our long-standing relationship, there are times I feel a little estranged from him. I know you must be wondering - how does someone feel estranged from a person you can't see, hear or share a sandwich with? Well, all I can say to that is when you're used to having someone around, someone who tells you cool stuff in your head, someone whose life you've read about and studied, and who you think you understand and who you believe understands you, someone who you can't help but respect and admire for the way he conducted himself when he was here having a shot at this life thing, and suddenly you realize that person isn't as much part of your life as they were a little while ago, it's not a nice feeling. Like when I realize my husband and I haven't kissed on the mouth for a while. Just...*not right.* And with Jesus, I always know who moved. It's never Jesus that backs off. I back off. I go away. I go inside. I go outside. I go off. I go around. I get busy. I get lazy. I get angry. I get suicidal. I become afraid. I become conceited. I have success. I have failure. I lose focus. I lose sleep. I get my period. I get a new friend.

And Jesus just waits. And eventually, I get back around to him, because I know He's what's missing.

So I've been really low this time. *Really low.* This time, it's been harder, because all the stuff I usually use to prop myself up is gone. I'm unemployed. I've put the weight I lost last year back on again. We have no money in the bank. I have nothing to show for this year. But I did say that this year was not going to be a year for having something to show. This year was for Ben, to give him a chance to show. And it's been good for that reason. But it's been hard, having nothing to show. What we have to show is a marriage that works, and considering what we've been through, that's a lot. But in the bigger picture, to the rest of the world we live in, that's really the least we could do. A functional marriage shouldn't be anything special, it should be a basic. So we are twenty-two years married, and still just doing basics. It's hard not to feel discouraged sometimes.

And it's at times like these I miss my friend.

So, my usual time to talk to Jesus is when I'm in bed, before I go to sleep. We might be there an hour, maybe a minute. I love that time, because it's so quiet, and there's no distractions or demands. I've nowhere to go, nothing to take my attention away. A few days ago, I asked him to talk to me. It's been so long since I heard your voice, can't you talk to me? How do I hear you? Where are you?

And Jesus said "In the beginning was the Word, and the Word was with God, and the Word was God. He was with God in the beginning." 1 John 1: 1 and 2. *I was there in the beginning Jo, outside of time, with God, back when it began. If I can be there with Him, then I can be here with you now. I was there, and I'm here.*

The next night. *Jesus. I want to feel you. I want to see you. How do I feel you, see you? I hunger for your substance, not just for your voice inside me.* And Jesus said "Through him all things were made; without him nothing was made that has been made." 1 John 1:3. *I made everything, Jo. Everything is here because of me. I was there with God at creation, making everything. You can hear me, see me, feel me. Listen. Look around you. Touch the things I've made. I'm here with you.*

And I listened. I could hear rain falling into the creek just a few metres away, outside our bedroom window. I could hear frogs and crickets

75

speaking, singing. I could hear air moving the trees. I heard him. All of the things he made sounded just like him, sounded of him. When I listened for him, I heard him.

He is close. He's always close. He speaks. He's always all around. I don't know how he talks to me the way he does, but he does. If you don't believe, that's okay. I don't believe sometimes either. But even when I lose my grip on him he never loses his grip on me. I love Jesus. He's a good friend.

10

Looking For The God-Shaped Hole

The God-Shaped hole.

Have you ever heard of the theory of the God-shaped hole? It goes something like this.

"People who don't know God have a God-shaped hole inside them that only He can fill. That's why everyone who isn't a Christian is always chasing something – they need something to go in the hole, because it hurts. Our job as Christians is to bring people to church so they can find out what's missing in their lives, and get God into their God-shaped hole."

The God-shaped hole.

What is the God-shaped hole? Is it really the sense of hopelessness a person feels when they don't know or understand God? Is there really a void in the soul that constantly needs filling, and it this truly the reason why people become addicts and workaholics, why they fill their lives with things and entertainment and sex and thrills? Is it really a space only God himself can actually fit into? If a God-shaped hole really is a place where God, and the things that matter to God can't reach, whose fault is that?

I think we're looking in the wrong place for the God-shaped hole. The God shaped hole isn't inside people. The God shaped hole *is* people.

The God shaped-hole is a void where God is absent.

The God-shaped hole is where ever God wills something to be, and yet, it isn't there. A God-shaped hole is a place where God longs to exist, but where there's actually no evidence of him. A God-shaped hole is what happens in the place wherever God's will is and where that will goes unheeded, unpracticed, unfulfilled, unheard or undone.

It's us.

The God-shaped hole actually happens when God's people don't do what God's will is. It isn't just something that's inside people who don't know God. Whenever we choose not to act upon God's will for others, but instead act only on God's will for ourselves, we are the God-shaped hole.

Where God wills change, and there is no change, there is the God-shaped hole.

Where God wills health, and no hand brings healing, there is the God-shaped hole.

Where God wills a hungry belly filled, and a hungry belly remains, there is the God-shaped hole.

Where God wills a family restored, and a family stays broken, there is the God-shaped hole.

Where God wills an addict be freed, and an addict remains ensnared, there is the God-shaped hole.

Where God wills a child be protected, and a child is abused, there is the God-shaped hole.

When God wills a kind word or deed, and the word remains unspoken, there is the God-shaped hole.

Where God wills acceptance, yet judgment remains, there is the God-shaped hole.

Where God wills the prodigals joyous homecoming, yet the prodigal finds the door closed and bolted, there is the God-shaped hole.

Where God wills community, and yet people see only each other's differences, there is the God-shaped hole.

Where God wills love, and yet there are envy, boasting and pride, anger, rudeness, records of wrongs, and delight in evil, there, right there, is the God-shaped hole.

The God-shaped hole is not in the person who doesn't know God and acts to relieve himself of his suffering. The God-shaped hole is in the one who does know God, yet never seeks to relieve another's suffering. It's time we stopped looking outside of ourselves for the problems of this world. We are the problems of this world. If we see others as bereft, because they don't have God, and yet do nothing to assist them in their pain, or seek to solve the world's problems, what does that make us?

11

Everything I Ever Needed To Know About Life

I Learned From ABBA

Yesterday afternoon, my husband grabbed the kids and a couple of beach towels and made for the car. I was about to go and change into my swimmers too when I picked up the remote and pointed it at the TV to turn it off. Suddenly, my whole childhood flashed before me. It was the first few scenes of ABBA - The Movie. Not Mamma Mia, the appallingly twee 2008 cinema release starring Meryl Streep and Pierce Brosnan which I refused to pay money to see purely on principle, but *the real ABBA - The Movie,* filmed in 1977 to coincide with the Swedish supergroups Australian tour.

When I recognized the opening credits, I felt a little gasp pop out of my mouth, and I got that twang you get in the back of your jaw when you're about to burst into tears. My husband stopped in the doorway and opened his mouth to ask if I was coming to the beach, but when he saw what was on TV, he just rolled his eyes and said, "We'll be back for dinner".

I then sat back and immersed myself in my own personal kind of bliss for ninety-five minutes, excluding ads. I reveled in the thinly plotted pseudo-documentary, following an Australian radio host as he tries desperately to interview ABBA during their hectic tour. I'm led to believe the director, Lasse Hallström, who also directed most of the bands film clips, made up the plot for the film on the plane on the way to Australia to shoot it. It shows, but I don't care.

I giggled helplessly watching girls the same age as I was back then in their own home-made ABBA t-shirts, created using those free iron-on transfers they used to give us in the Sunday papers. I longingly admired all those glossy, flicked bangs and high-waisted Lee's, squealing right along with a thousand twelve year old girls waving their crepe paper banners. I thought I held my excitement pretty well in check until the familiar piano glissando that is the first few bars of Dancing Queen. Then I completely lost it. I sobbed like the nine year old I was in 1977, when I, like a million other preteen Australian girls, swung my long, blonde Agnetha locks around on my imaginary dance floor between my bed and the dressing table mirror, *having the time of my life*. One day, when I turned the magical seventeen, I swore that I too would stalk those ubiquitous dance floors, looking for the right music, looking for my dancing king. Days of innocence indeed. By the time we girls actually turned seventeen in the eighties it was pretty clear that while we had been listening to ABBA, the boys had been listening to their older brothers Rod Stewart and Rolling Stones. Try telling a seventeen year old guy who's just cornered his first pash at the blue-light disco that we were *supposed* to leave them burning and then be gone. Oh ABBA, you should have been a whole session on your own in Personal Development in high school.

As I watched them yesterday afternoon on TV, in their ridiculous disco-pirate-flapper-glam clothes and their day-glow paint-box makeup, I felt a little embarrassed at how much I adore them. Unlike pop-concerts these days, in 1977 pop audiences were populated not with scantily dressed teenage girls, or gawping teen boys, but with *families* - grandparents, little kiddies, housewives doing the bump with each other and dads waving sparklers with their spotty, prepubescent sons. Thirty or so years later, watching Anna and Agnetha vamping it up onstage, I realized a little shocked that ABBA were actually a little bit *trampy*. Why had I never seen it before? And all those kids - the boys and girls, teens and parents and grannies - were lapping it all up with relish, despite the fact it looks today a bit like The Wiggles meets Lady Gaga.

More than just a musical obsession, ABBA was for me also a favourite childhood game. ABBA is played like this. You need a) one bossy girl to be the blonde singer Agnetha, b) a friend prepared to be the dark haired and slightly less popular Frida, and c) at least one younger brother, preferably two, willing to be Benny and Bjorn. You'll also need two hairbrushes for microphones, a tape recorder with batteries, a tennis racket for a guitar and an adjustable flat surface like an ironing board for Benny to play piano on. You also need a stage. My family lived in a new housing estate at the end of a cul de sac, where every other house was an empty exhibition home. And every one of those houses had a cement porch out front. So, bossy lead singer organises venue, hasty rehearsal and play list ensues, while slightly harried Frida sequesters wardrobe from her mums' collection of hot-pants and handkerchief tops. Bjorn, using the one hand left free from his tennis racket guitar, pops cassette into tape recorder and presses play...voila - hours of Eurovision-contest-style fun. I spent a year playing this game and never tired of it, which perhaps had something to do with the fact I always got to be Agnetha. But you know what? I was learning important leadership skills. ABBA was probably in fact the most profound educational influence I was ever exposed to. More importantly, my ABBA game taught me how to convincingly win talent contests and perform exhilarating karaoke.

ABBA actually opened me up to a whole world I never knew existed. They sang songs about far away places and political events I'd never heard of in primary school. I mean, who knew there was a country called Sweden before ABBA won Eurovision? Who had ever heard of *Eurovision*? And I ask you, how many nine-year olds these days know about Waterloo? And without Fernando, would we have ever known of a Mexican Revolution, or a place called the Rio Grande? ABBA's songs encompassed a virtual plethora of culture, history and geography. Back in the seventies, ABBA and their songs opened up the world for us way before there was ever Google or the Discovery Channel.

And the world of geography and culture wasn't the only one ABBA opened up for we pre-internet tweenies. If I learned anything important from ABBA, it was the about the complexities of human relationships. Before Agnetha and Bjorn, I had never actually known anyone who *got a divorce*. The relationships between those four band members swung wildly from the dizzy limerance of I Do, I Do, I Do and Mamma Mia to the dark melancholy of My Love, My Life and Knowing Me, Knowing You. As a young girl, watching the slow deterioration of those two made-in-heaven marriages, I realised that the real world was far from a platform-heeled, platinum-permed, picture perfect place.

I think one of the things I love the most about ABBA is that they absolutely embodied everything I thought I ever wanted in life. Glittery eye-shadow. Satin pedal-pushers. Singing on a stage in front of everybody. For some of us, dressing up and being in front of people just having the time of your life is the exemplification of sheer joy. Belying the fact that Frida was opera trained, and Agnetha was a well-known and renowned folk singer in

Sweden before they ever became ABBA, what I love most about their singing is that *anyone can join in*. And it makes you smile to do it. It's not this moany speak-singing which typifies so many folk artists today, nor is it the impossible technical fluctuations of your Celine, Christina or Mariah. I love ABBA because ABBA made me think singing and music was something *I could do*. These days, Idol-style television competitions have meant that singing has become so incredibly technical as to be physically impossible to emulate for most normal people. Perhaps I'm just getting old and cranky, but I believe great singers and musicians don't just make a platform for themselves - great artists make their stage into an experience we can all enjoy. They make it so we think "You know what? I love that, and I can do it too, and we can all do it together, and it's all gonna be so much fun." Back in the seventies, ABBA invited a million nine year olds just like me, and their bumping mothers and gawping brothers and grinning grandparents, to stand up and sing along. ABBA gave us simple music with catchy melodies we could all remember, and guess what? They were so good we still remember them, and we still sing today. Contemporary artists, take note, especially if your goal is to bring lasting joy to people all over the world for generations to come.

ABBA sang to me when I was young and idealistic of optimism, hope, aspiration and joy, while I danced on the porch and mimed every single word they wrote into my hairbrush. I did then, and will always, dream of a world where women can be as innocent, free, sensual and un-self-conscious as the Dancing Queen, and not be exploited, abused or denigrated somehow. And when ABBA sang about getting your own money in a rich mans world, I always considered it much more a call to arms than a groan of resignation.

ABBA also taught me, in my most impressionable of years, that there was a bigger world out there, a world filled with joy and fun that must be enjoyed now, because it doesn't last forever. ABBA demonstrated in blazing colour that fame and friendships and marriages can fade and even break, pop stars can become recluses and even the most wonderful music can be stripped of all it's magic and made into mindless pap. Nothing lasts forever, it's true, but ABBA the phenomenon will go on and on. *I hope.*

ABBA – bless their little skin tight pedal-pushers – have also made those who truly love them almost as famous as they ever were. We ABBA fans are a whole generation now renowned for both their excellent taste in music and their questionable taste in clothes. ABBA, I thank *you* for the music, because you were the greatest childhood a kid ever had.

12

Love Means Never Having To Say

I'm Not The One Who's the Alcoholic

I don't drink. Alcohol, that is. I stopped drinking December 2009. Before that, I liked to drink, and did so whenever I liked. Not too much, you understand, just a glass of red or two probably five nights a week, and sometimes the whole bottle, except for the last half a glass I'd toddle over and tip down the sink swearing not to do it again the next night. I don't quite know how I ended up with that habit. I think it was medicinal, and probably started around the same time my husbands drinking did. I started drinking myself to cope with the issues that arose from the fact my husband was drinking a lot. And he was drinking a lot. In the end, he had to leave, because his alcoholism was driving me to something resembling it and more besides. He went away to rehab, actually, and to his credit, he sorted it out, with a lot of help. He's back home now and things are grand.

While he was away at rehab, I used the solace and privacy as an opportunity to do a bit of therapeutic drinking. I'm fairly sure this is how I carried on the whole time he was gone. I now see the unfairness and hypocrisy of it, but my excuse was that I was not the alcoholic, he was, and technically, it was true. But if he had a problem with drink, then *we* had a problem with drink, and not just my drinking or his drinking, but the reasons we thought drinking could help whatever was wrong with us. It wasn't my husband - it wasn't even the drinking that was the real issue. There were, as is usually the case in dysfunctional, codependent, enabling relationships, deeper problems we had no capacity to face up to which were the problem. Drinking was just anesthetic, avoidance, staggering around, slurring-of-the-speech suspension of animation.

My husband has no memory of vast sections of the two years he was drinking heavily. Significant events are missing from his recollection–moving house, holidays, big decisions that were made and conversations that were pivotal in our life. I'd say they were gone from his memory, but I doubt they really ever went in. They came at him and rebounded clean off his consciousness like a poorly aimed beer bottle thrown at a bin. We have sections of our married life that he was physically present for, but which he conducted in some kind of mental, emotional and spiritual automatic state; his real self was trapped in a world of pain inside his chest, inside his head. I see I was right in my perception that back then he was simply not all there. He was a personality perfectly preserved, pickled for posterity in a brown glass bottle.

The month he came home from rehab, we went along to his prospective boss' Christmas Party - a flash soiree on a charter boat. The bar was open and gratis to all. We discussed it beforehand, and knew it would be his first real test. But he did great. I'd decided I wouldn't drink at the party to show my support, although we didn't talk about the issue of whether I would drink in the future, and if I did, how that was going to work. While we were at the party, my husband bumped into a guy who'd been in the rehab a few months before he had. He was working for the company my husband would be working for, and doing well. He too was finding it hard with the alcohol flowing freely all around us, and no way to get off the boat, but he was holding up manfully. He had his partner with him. She had a beer bottle in one hand, and a glass of wine in the other – both for herself. The pressure on her man to keep up his bargain with God and with himself was his alone to bear. She told me "Well, why not? *I'm* not the one who's the alcoholic, am I?"

It was then I decided I didn't need to drink any more.

Over the past year, friends have invited me out with them, touting it as my chance to imbibe independent of my 'dry' husband, a chance to *really enjoy myself,* as if going out and not drinking were the equivalent of bathing in public in a vat of cold porridge. I sincerely thank them; I'm not as much offended by the fact they want to sneak me out to drink behind my husbands back as I am disheartened. I guess the fact that we had such a long road to reconcile our marriage just brings this whole element of loyalty to the issue. As hard as it was for me to allow a sneaky, lying drunk back into the house, it must have been just as hard for him to come back to a distrustful, anxiety ridden female. I think my teetotalling is the least I can do to show him 1) I'm not frightened of him anymore and 2) we're actually doing this thing together.

It's been a year, and it hasn't been hard for me – the drinking part at least. For my husband, it's been harder, and it's an ongoing journey. God's grace is all we have going for us, and we see it every day extended toward us in ways we could never have imagined, great and small. We are happy and love each other so much, more than we ever have or had the capacity to in the 22 years we've been married. It's been said that he who has been forgiven much loves much, and both my husband and I appreciate how much the other had to forgive for this present happiness to exist. We each have been given a great gift, precious, and to be treated with respect and deference. He is a drunk redeemed by mercy...I am a shrew redeemed by giving it.

My husband being an alcoholic, and my potential to follow him, is not as big a deal now, but it certainly was when it was with us. I won't easily forget finding spirit bottles refilled with cold tea and water, seeing him drive up with our son in the car and a beer bottle between his thighs, or stumbling across secret caches of empty beer bottles or finding a wine bottle with one glass left in it at the back of the cupboard, months after he'd gone away to rehab…and realising I must have been the one who hid it.

There but for the grace of God.

13

It's Okay Not To Love Your Church

*"I just **love** my church!"*

A lot of my friends on Facebook put this up as their status update pretty often. Other variations might be "*My church is so **awesome**!*" "*Hey, wasn't the preaching this morning jus*t ***mind-blowing**?*" or "*Just love being in the '**house**'!*" I think I know why they do it, because I've done it too. We do it to make people who read it feel like they're missing out on something by not being at church, because we wish they'd come. I don't know if it works, and I don't want to be all cynical and say it never could be effective in causing someone to feel like they would like to go to church, because who knows? Stranger things have happened.

What I wanted to say about this is that it's actually okay if you don't say this about your church, and it's even okay if you don't feel this way. You might not "love" your church after all. You might feel ambivalent about church at times, and that's all right. I feel that way about my husband and kids at times, and it doesn't mean we don't belong together.

Hey, if putting "My church is so ***awesome**!*" up on your Facebook status floats your boat, go for it. I would like to say though that in my experience, the people who don't go to your church that read your status update on how much you love it pretty much couldn't care less if you like church, love it or loathe it. It makes no difference to them whatsoever. If they think church is uncool, you saying you love it probably isn't going to change their minds.

Now before you send me hate mail, can I just say I do love my church...sometimes. There are moments, days and weeks that church annoys the heck out of me. I used to love church a lot more when I went to one that had flashing lights, a great audio visual fest and tight-as-a-drum music team providing the music, because that's what I really like and enjoy. But we don't go to that kind of church any more. We go to a church now that is good at other things, and it's been kind of hard to adapt, but overall, it suits us better. Our old church used to provide a huge emotional burst on Sunday mornings, and with it a strong sense of church culture, church identity and church affinity. But our new church isn't as good at creating that. This church does a lot of things for people who don't go to the church, whom the community generally consider to be what we in Australia would call "rat-bags" – people who drink a lot, people who take drugs, people who can't hold down jobs, people who can't sustain relationships, and people who don't fit into other churches. They also open the church to groups from other ethnic groups to hold their own services in their own languages. All this probably sounds great on paper, but it's not as glamourous as it sounds. Sometimes, the rat-bags don't know how to behave in church or as church, and sometimes they come and take whatever is given to them and leave and never come back, or never seem to change, or they get saved and then backslide and they hook up with each other and make us all frustrated and cranky. And the people from other ethnicities hang in their own little groups in church and don't mix much, funnily, just like the rest of us. And even the people who come every week don't ever seem to change...just like the worship music. It's not a huge catalogue we have – consistent I guess you'd call it. But you know what? It's all okay. It's the church, after all, and the church is people, and we *all* know about *people*.

No, sometimes I don't love my church. And I don't know much of the time if they love me, mainly because I don't know how to trust in a love I can't feel, and because I'm not used to being loved and not being able to *feel* it. I guess that's what faith is – believing in a love you've been told is there, but that you can't necessarily feel. Sometimes, I don't feel like I love my husband too, and sometimes I don't feel his love for me, but that doesn't mean it isn't there. This thing I don't always feel holds us together, he and I, and we have learned a lot about love from loving each other. By the way, when I tell people I love my husband, it's because I want them to know he and I are lovers, not because I want them to come partake of the love for themselves. This is why I don't think it really works, this telling people you love your church as a way of turning people onto it For your unchurched friends, it's probably something like sitting next to your best friend at the movies while she pashes a guy you think is a creep - a bit awkward, and not the least bit tempting.

Don't worry about selling your church to your friends. And don't worry if you can't tell people you love your church because you're not sure you actually do. I'm not worried any more about my ambivalence toward the church, because like my relationships, my involvement in church probably shouldn't be based on whether it makes me happy, or makes me feel loved, or gives me identity or affinity or purpose. It's a commitment. My involvement in church is rooted in knowing the church is Jesus' body, and it's where we belong. And just like I am committed to caring affectionately for, being devoted to and giving myself to my husbands body, I care affectionately for, am devoted to and give myself to the body of Christ – the church – even if at times it doesn't meet my needs, make me feel good, or do what I wish it would. Even if it doesn't please me the ways I like to be pleased. Even if it doesn't…heaven forbid… make me happy. You never find a perfect church anyway…you only ever find one with problems you're prepared to put up with. It's okay not to love your church sometimes. Feelings come and go, and love is more than how you feel anyway. Love is what you do. I love the church in that I consider myself a part of it and I can't ever see a time when I won't be part of it. But I don't tell people I love my church much, not as much as I used to. I don't know anyone I might need to convince of it. Including myself.

14

Supermarket Shopping at ALDI –

A Study In Very Peculiar Human Behaviour

I shop at ALDI. I don't love to shop there, but I do prefer it to the other available supermarkets. ALDI appeals to me on many levels. I like the fact that ALDI has only three aisles in the whole store, and I can reach and see everything because it's almost all stacked on the floor. I like that ALDI has virtually one choice in each grocery item – one brand of peanut butter, one brand of meat pie, one brand of bread. And I like that they're cheaper than every other supermarket. I like simplicity, and I like my shopping done fast, and ALDI is simplicity and speed exemplified. You go in the front door, you go up and down the aisles, and you exit through the checkout. Simple. No browsing, no dawdling, no brainer. But then it must be said that I am one of those people who, in other supermarkets, uses the self-serve checkout because I can't stand the way others scan and pack my purchases. I do it faster and I do it neater. *I do it*…and that's all the reason I need. It's a control thing. Yes, it's likely I was traumatised in the past. Maybe it's because my father used to manage a Woolworths store. How Freudian.

ALDI is for people who like control. ALDI works for control freaks because so much of what happens there is completely up to you. ALDI don't have trolley collectors – they have trolley tokens. They don't have customer service – they have about four staff in the whole store at one time doing everything from placing out stock to operating checkouts. ALDI don't do your head in with marketing – you never need fear you've been manipulated into buying something, because there is no merchandising whatsoever. At ALDI, no one tries to make you comfortable, and no one caters for your shopping or personal needs. ALDI just wants you to get your needs in the trolley and go on your way. ALDI is not so much a shopping experience as it is a social experiment. It reminds me quite a lot of high school - as long as you know your way around, and work out quickly how not to piss anyone off, you manage just fine.

Shopping in ALDI is quite a different experience from shopping in other supermarkets. It's not for the kind of shopper who likes to browse up and down aisles, taking things down and reading labels and comparing prices. ALDI is not for people who might go grocery shopping to fill up an empty afternoon. ALDI is not for people who like to have a checkout person pack their things in bags while they watch, flicking through their store cards and lay-by dockets. ALDI is also not for the old, infirm or for people who have a heart condition. However, if ALDI lacks sophistication, it certainly makes up for it in complexity. It only looks simpler because the usual shopping rules don't apply. ALDI shoppers are not mere customers perusing a retail landscape – they are highly skilled retail commandos negotiating a hostile environment.

ALDI shoppers are resolutely on a mission. They know that no one is there to take care of them if they become lost or confused. They know that at any time, they might be injured or separated from their loved ones. They understand that what they see in front of them is all that is available in the store. They do not meander, and they do not browse. They do not pause or hesitate or compare brands or prices. ALDI shoppers drive their trolleys like armoured recovery vehicles, directing them straight up one aisle and down the other with one hand as they sequester supplies with the other. ALDI shoppers do not need to stop to look for what they want – they know the store layout backwards, literally. Experienced ALDI shoppers stop their trolleys for only two reasons; either because they need both hands to grab more stuff, or because some uninitiated non- ALDI person has stopped in front of them to look for another brand of coffee or cheaper two-minute noodles. Experienced ALDI shoppers sigh out loud a lot – it helps stop to them from kicking other people in the backs of the knees.

ALDI shoppers are always anxious during their expeditions, because they know they cannot choose another brand of something if what they want has been sold out. Nobody wants to go back to ALDI another day to grab just a couple of things, because ALDI checkouts are not like normal checkouts. There are no express lanes. Because of this there is an unwritten code concerning what happens when someone just has a few things to buy, which is as follows. The person who has a few things must stand quietly behind the person in front of them who has a trolley load, and wait until they are noticed. They must not do anything to draw attention to themselves so that they can be hurried through, like clear their throats loudly, or ask to be let through ahead of everyone else. They must wait for the discretion of the person with many things, who is free to ignore them if they wish. After all, they have just completed a successful mission requiring a high level of skill, whereas the person with the few things clearly is very poorly organised if they had to come back for something in between missions. *Amateurs.* Now, if you're the person with the full trolley, it is okay to let one or even two people go in front of you (never three, that's going too far), if that will make you feel good on that particular day, but you are under no obligation to do so. Full trolley people have the power. They may relinquish that power, or not, and if you are the person with a few things, there's nothing you can do about it, except smile sheepishly and say thank you if access is granted, or else suck it up and wait if it is not. One day you will be the one with the power, and you will understand that this is just the way it is.

Once, I saw someone with a few things just walk to the front of the queue and put their things down without waiting to be invited to do so. There was an audible gasp, and angry glances were exchanged. Other people with a few things saw their big chance, and a couple almost made a break for it, but we full-trolleyed people quickly subdued them with our collective, silent outrage. If the person who barged to the front of the queue hadn't been a very large and menacing-looking man who apparently didn't speak any English he would have been subjected to a full and very indignant explanation of the checkout etiquette right there and then, I can tell you.

ALDI is cheap, and it's been proven that overall they are cheaper than every other supermarket in Australia. But don't think ALDI customers don't pay for it in other ways. ALDI is not for people who like their food cupboards to reflect their socio-economic status. If you shop at ALDI, your pantry will look like it's stocked with kiddie groceries, the kind made from grey plastic to look like tins with colourful labels and absurd made-up brand names on them. You will also come home from the supermarket with bruised shins. You will become the kind of person who goes crazy when someone takes your trolley token out of the change tray in your car, mistaking it for a two-dollar coin. You will take pride in sharing the best chocolate available in any supermarket in this country with your friends (ALDI sells the most sublime chocolate) but then you will be obliged to reveal to them where you bought it when they announce they too must have it. And this is a problem, because while ALDI shoppers are seasoned experts, they are also obliged to be discreet about it. ALDI shoppers do not enjoy the social status associations that Coles or Woolworths shoppers do. Like public housing, or insulin, you probably wouldn't choose ALDI if you thought you really had a choice.

Because of this, ALDI dedicates can be closed books when it comes to revealing their supermarket shopping loyalties, and it could be because they actually possess a secret life – an alternative personality that reveals itself only in the brutally frugal atmosphere of the local ALDI store. Their true and usually well-hidden financial, emotional and psychological condition is revealed and played out for that one-half hour every week when they venture out for the weekly grocery shop. You can pretend you are socially adept, well-adjusted and on top of your game in every other sphere, but if you shop at ALDI, I can tell you who and what you really are. Number one – you are cheap. Two – you are probably a bit mad. And three – you are definitely a *survivor*.

15

Nine Things Tenants Want Their Landlords to Know.

We are renters, have been for over ten years now. The great thing about renting is that when the house you live in has issues – like a bathroom floor that leaks or a bit of back yard that suspiciously never quite dries out properly, you can either merrily ignore it, or else if you're feeling especially fussy, report it to your real estate agent. When you're a renter, most of the things that go wrong around the house are *someone else's problem.* The downside of renting is that your lovely home, your retreat from the world and the place you keep all that's important to you in the world, pretty much amounts in reality to someone else's second priority. When times get tough, an investment property is the first thing to get let go. Hot water services don't get fixed, fences don't get replaced and, worst possible case scenario, homes get sold right out from underneath tenants, even the loyal, tidy, diligent on-time rent-paying ones.

But we tenants want landlords to know we do appreciate you and your investment immensely. I love renting and don't envisage stopping any time soon, so I have a vested interest in being a good tenant. I clean up after myself, I pay my rent on time, I report any problems and I allow access whenever I can. And because I am a good tenant, I would like to take this opportunity to tell landlords a few things tenants wish they knew. Here goes.

1) Please don't put cream, beige, eggshell, ecru, bone, off-white or heaven forbid, white coloured carpet in your investment property, even if it's cheap. There's a reason why it's cheap. Your tenant will not be able to keep that carpet clean, no matter what lengths they go to. Even if they are able to by some miracle, at some stage they will have a visitor who will bring to your property a child with gastro, a shaken up bottle of Fanta, an incontinent pet and a large, runny and violently coloured jelly dessert, and your tenant will be powerless to stop them. Just go for a nice shade of grey - it covers a multitude of sins.

2) If your investment property is over fifteen years old, please do not expect your tenant to remove dirt so old it can be carbon dated.

3) Timber floors get scratched. Please do not penalise your tenants for putting furniture, walking or breathing on the timber floor. If you want to keep those timber floors scratch-free, put carpet down over them, and how's about you make it a nice shade of grey.

4) Ovens and stoves are important. This is because tenants will want to eat every day, preferably food they cooked in the house they pay to live in. It's

therefore important to your tenant that they have more than two square feet of useable bench space, and that the stove and oven work properly. Note - if the appliances in question were manufactured before 1975 and been used by thirty sets of tenants since then, they don't work properly.

5) Vertical blinds are in no way legitimate window coverings. They are ten kinds of stupid and bare-butt ugly. Vertical blinds fall down, become tangled and get grubby whenever a butterfly stretches its wings a continent away. Put up cheap tab-top curtains, cover the windows with newspaper for crying out loud, but please, do not put up vertical blinds, unless you want to wake up with a horse's head on your pillow.

6) If your investment property has more than two bedrooms, there is a very good chance we will probably want to bring our children to live there with us. Children are those small people who do not understand lease agreements, vertical blinds and cream coloured carpet, and having your property manager scowl fractiously at mine every time they visit doesn't really help.

7) Insect screens are not made to last forever. They have holes in them because they were last replaced in 1983. We didn't destroy them; they were so decimated by age that one day, a fly just flew straight through one and didn't even stop.

8) I love the aubergine feature wall on the landing, really I do, but you only have to walk within three feet to take a chip out of it you can see from across the street. That would actually have made a great carpet colour. Next time, if you just reverse all your wall/carpet colour choices, we'll be sweet.

9) When you decide you want to sell your investment property slash my home, I do not become excited by the prospect of having photos taken of my possessions while I am packing to get out with three weeks notice, or having an open house on the day the removalist is coming, or having someone just pop back to check the colour of the bathroom tiles while I am trying to untangle your vertical blinds and having Fanta professionally steam cleaned from your cream coloured carpet. I just gave you a big pile of my money to give to your bank. Give me just a small break. Please.

Thank you, thank you, thank you to all you landlords who have decided to invest in property. Because of you, I have been able to live in some lovely homes; and to me they have been homes, while to you they were probably just houses. Homes are lived in. Houses are tenanted. If you have an investment property, you don't want just a tenant. You want someone like me - someone who loves the house they live in, takes care of it as if it as their own. By the way, if you have a four-bedder with a dishwasher vacant in Newcastle you're trying to lease, give me a call, will you?

16

Bringing Up Teenagers Whilst Retaining My Sanity –

Don't Ask Me, I Haven't Done It Yet

I am evil. While at several stages of my life I had fleeting thoughts that perhaps I had the capacity to be so, I know now that it's true. I have witnesses. Every day I am forced to confront several people who not only tell me I am possessed by the darkest kind of depraved wrongness, but are able to argue quite convincingly for their case. Thusly, I am persuaded it's true. Who are these people? They are my teenage children.

In order to support their position, I give you the following evidence. First, I have been known on occasion to ask them to wash dishes while they are still eating food I lovingly prepared and set carefully in front of them on said dishes. *Evil.* Also, I have at particular times requested that they take a pile of their clothes which I washed, dried and folded for them to their rooms to be put away in the drawers I paid for with my own money, and I asked pretty please could they try to keep those clothes in the same state of neatness for the whole of the journey. *Evil, evil, evil.* I have also had the brazen audacity to provide a decent education for each of them, and then queried whether they wanted to use said education in order to further them in their lives in some way, or even just to move from my couch to the bus queue in order that they may find gainful employment. *I don't know how I can stand myself.* I even told one of them they couldn't go out to a friends place three nights in a row. *I know.* I need to find an exorcist, or at least a therapist with a penchant for dealing with the especially twisted kind of sadistic nastiness I am clearly afflicted by.

Further proof of my evilness are the times I have become angry upon finding my change purse was missing all the gold ones I was saving up for something nice just for me. Then there are the times I've shown resistance to their asking for the last few dollars I had in the whole world, because I might have wanted to selfishly buy myself a coffee one day while I was out of the house, free albeit briefly from folding and washing. What was I thinking? Clearly, not about them. And then there was when I had the hide to ask them for a few dollars of their money to pay for the petrol I had to use to drive them to their friends house or the beach or the shopping mall. I suppose I should have thought about whether I planned to keep on being so selfish way back when I got pregnant. Some people just shouldn't be allowed to have children.

Other transgressions of mine include asking the boyfriend/girlfriend of my child to come inside and say hello to myself and their father. I know now this is like asking them if they would like to clip their granny's rancid

ingrown toenails, and is likely to produce the exact same vomit reflex.
Equally sinful is my asking their father for a second opinion on something
I've already said yes to, (tantamount to changing my mind about something
to their disadvantage, which is worse than murder) and, worst of all, having
sex with their father and liking it. How they know I did this last one I'm
sure I don't know. The fact I'm not the least bit sorry for it or ashamed of it
further compounds my wickedness. I don't know how I can stand myself.

I've worked out that worrying about or being concerned for them is also
very, very wrong - I've been told I *don't have to do it*, so why on earth
would I, and seeing as I can't seem to help it, I must be mentally
incompetent as well as evil. Lying in bed at three in the morning, imagining
all kinds of unspeakable things happening to my babies - I must have a
very depraved mind, they tell me, to be able to think such things could ever
happen out there in the big, bright, beautiful world, filled as it is with
rainbows and butterflies. You can do anything and go anywhere mum, as
long as you stay innocent and see the world as a beautiful place and all
people as truly beautiful. Angus and Julia Stone said so, so it must be true,
and besides nothing bad has apparently ever happened to them other than
these broken teenaged hearts they seem to always be singing about. Broken
hearts, even the kind that render a teen absolutely speechless with
emotional distress, are apparently secret teenagers business, and absolutely

off-limits for discussion. I've been told *I just wouldn't understand.*

Don't worry about me, they admonish, as if I had committed some crime by assuming someone I share half my genes with was my ongoing concern. A vivid imagination is forerunner of insanity, so I'd better watch myself, they say. I bet institutions are full of crazy, evil mothers who allowed their imaginations to run away with them, and their live, healthy offspring are all grown-up, safe and healthy and happy and prosperous, far away from the car wrecks and roadside ditches of this world. Only a truly wicked mind could think so clever and discerning a child with such thoughtful and responsible friends could ever end up any other way. Ah me - is there no hope of redemption?

When it comes to trying to do what's best with my teenagers, it seems I'm damned no matter what I do. I've tried explaining I'd rather argue with them than face a police officer at the door with his cap in his hand, but they think those things only happen on T.V. I've tried negotiating with them, because I know full well that things do go wrong and errors of judgment do happen, and part of a parents job is to fix things when they go wrong, and take responsibility for the consequences of their children's actions. But my teenagers, well, they think the problems is not with the world, with the odds, with other people who don't love them as much as me, or who don't care who they hurt, or with wet roads and speeding cars and bad choices...they think the problem is *with me*. Sometimes I feel like all that stands between them and potential disaster is my being the bad guy one more time, and I do feel bad when I have to say no. My teenagers would have me believe my bad feelings exist because I'm not supposed to say no, and I should alleviate my self-imposed distress by saying *yes, many more times*. That's because they have never pushed a little baby out of their body for eight hours. They don't know that sometimes feeling very, very bad comes at the same time as doing something very, very good. Like telling your child they can't get in a car to go *God knows where* at 10.30pm with someone who won't even give you his Christian name. But what the hell would I know?

This evil that I have, I'm not sure I had it when they were small. When I herded them about the place as little ones I didn't feel like I was a bad parent if I had to pull them out of danger or grab them away from harms way. If I shouted "No!" as they were about to run in front of a bus, I didn't feel I needed to say sorry for it. They needed to feel my strength, my protection and my concern. But now, they don't want to feel those, and they don't even want to feel their own, even if it might keep them safe or healthy or take them places they want to go in this world. They hate it when they feel anything because of me. They want to butt up against the world first-hand now - feel the burn, the *whoosh* of the buss passing by too close, the stab in the heart from the unkind lover, the apprehension at the risk that may be just a little too far. They want to feel it, and I don't want them to, and for that, I must be punished.

I love my kids, and I know it's my lot to feel their resistance. I just wish they wouldn't make me feel it's wrong to worry about them and try to protect them. I wish I didn't have to think parental concern was a mental condition. And you know what? I wish, above everything, I could go back in time and treat my own mother the way I expect my teenagers to treat me at the moment. In an age before mobile phones and Facebook, I confess with total shame that my own mother must have been out of her mind with worry for me, the way I behaved. She could not have even fantasised about the scary, risky, stupid and dangerous things I got up to when I was my own kids age. She prayed I'd get the kids I deserved, and I laughed. Who says God doesn't hear mother's prayers?

To my own kids - guys, I love you. I know you love me. Forgive me my trespasses, as I always forgive yours. We'll get through this, one way or another. See you in the morning. xxx

17

Jesus, Emmanuel – God, At Ground Zero

It's March 18th. 2011. The earth is groaning. Floods. Cyclones. Earthquakes. And that's not all. Revolutions. Wars. Rumours of wars. My mind echoes with the booming words of preachers from my youth, warning that the days would come, the end-times - the words of God will ultimately be fulfilled in the time of this generation. But as I watch the T.V. reports of what is happening at the coalface of these disasters, the doomsday prophecies fade from my mind. All I see are people. Hurting people, terrified people, dying people, grieving people. Blood, water, flesh and earth, all mixed together. Everything that was built being demolished and washed away, wiped from the face of the earth. Everything that was made being unmade stretched, cracked and torn apart. Broken, lost and separated - people from one another, people from their possessions. And everything that once separated me from them – geography, income, gender, skin colour, beliefs, religion, culture – all of them mean nothing now. I reach out in my mind, in my spirit, across the distance and pray – God, be with them, God, your grace, God, please, a miracle, God, oh my God.

Where is God?

The doomsday prophets rise out of their chairs, go to their computers, press a button and begin their rants. They take up their pens and start to scrawl across the page. They sit, long into the night, combing their fingertips across the pages of their Bibles, straining, seeking the words that endorse their nightmarish visions. They climb the stairs to their ivory minarets and begin to call out - *thus sayeth the Lord, the judgment of God is visited upon you. God has shown his awesome power. God has sent His wrath, exacted His justice and sent the due penalty for your sin and your unrighteousness.*

The people do not look up. They are digging. They are searching. They are weeping, waiting and watching. They are praying – God, our God. Come to us. Wait with us. Watch with us. Bring breath to the lips of the breathless. Guide the hands of the helper, the healer, and the seeker. Comfort the mother, the father, the brother, the child. Grant the sinner time for his penitence. And help us, please, help us. If ever you could, God, please come now.

The prophet hears God in the blackness of his mind, muttering to him through the terrible imagery of the scriptures, speaking only to him. He hears God speak in his own, familiar voice – men are evil, men are damned, men cannot be trusted, men are unrighteous, fallen short, sinners. And God will not be mocked. He believes he is God's herald to other men. But it is still only ever his own voice he hears, in his own mind, in his own words, of his own conviction, in his own, empty room. Strange how God hates all the same people he does.

God has left him to it. God is out there, out at ground zero.

People want to know where God is, and He is there. He is down amongst them - weeping, pulling debris away, standing with someone as their loved one is carried free. God is offering His help, and making sure it is received where it's needed. God is speaking words of comfort. God is sending aid and support from a continent away. People say, we can't see God, we can't feel him. God should get himself down here; I'd like to give him a piece of my mind. People hear the prophets broadcast and they say if that is God, then we have no God. But God is, and He is there. And He knows. God came down and made himself flesh, and His flesh was broken. His possessions torn away. His family separated from Him. Everything He had was gone. God made flesh and flesh was decimated, and again and again flesh and earth and fire and water collide and God is at the heart, and walks with us, and weeps with us. Emmanuel. God with us.

In the maelstrom where men and their Creator meet, the conflict of ages, of sin and men and God and creation, colliding violently in disasters natural and sublime, mortal and spiritual, deliberate and elemental. We do not mean to hurt each another, or be hurt, yet hurt each other we do, and hurt we are. And the heart of God is as bruised by our pain as it is by our resistance.

Jesus is amongst us. He doesn't stand in a parapet and speak death and destruction over creation – He walks amongst us. Jesus is digging. He is searching. He is weeping, waiting and watching. He prays – God, my God. Come to them. Wait with them. Watch with them. Bring breath to the lips of the breathless. Comfort the mother, the father, the brother, the child. Guide the hands of the helper, the healer, and the seeker. Grant the sinner time for his penitence. Help them, please help them. You can help them – and so, I am here now.

"For God so loved the world that he gave his one and only Son, that whoever believes in him shall not perish but have eternal life. For God did not send his Son into the world to condemn the world, but to save the world through him. "John 3:16 and 17.

18

The Opposite Of Love

I remember a few years ago there was a discussion in Christian circles about exactly what the opposite of love could be. If people are not being kind and loving, what exactly were they doing instead? What do they need to *stop* doing so they *can* be loving, as we all know God is loving? What stops Christians, and those who aren't Christians, from loving their neighbours, and anyone else in their world for that matter? What is this key that might help Christians carry out 1 John 4:7 - *Let us love one another, for love comes from God* – so we could potentially stop wars, cure poverty and just generally help people get along? The rest of this scripture actually tells us that *everyone who loves has been born of God and knows God.* Love makes us like *Him*, because he *is* Love. Surely if we just did the opposite of whatever was preventing us from loving, we'd be heading in the right direction?

We'd all been assuming for ages that the opposite of love was hate. But then someone pointed out that you can hate someone and love someone at the same time, and that you can demonstrate hating behaviours directly towards someone you profess love for and vice versa. And we knew it was in fact quite possible to hold onto ones hate for someone or something and give all the outward appearances of love, or even to love just one sort of person and hate another sort for quite arbitrary reasons, if there were sufficient incentive to do so. So we stopped saying love and hate were opposites anymore, and resolved to just accept that in certain circumstances sometimes hating was unavoidable, and love impossible.

So after that, they said the opposite of love must be fear, because we only hate what we are afraid of, and once we know all about something and don't fear it any more we are able to love it. For example, Christians were encouraged to learn about and understand varying religious practices and sexual expressions in the hope that this would lead to greater capacity to love the people engaged in them. But unfortunately, 'others' remained 'others' despite everything we knew about them, the only difference being that Christians now knew more about the people they hated and could object to them in more personal and informed ways than ever was previously possible. Fear, it seemed, could not be eradicated by love, but fear could be useful in helping us work out who God's enemies were.

But then someone else said no, it isn't fear that's the opposite of love, it's actually indifference. And we all went "yeah!", because we could relate to being on the receiving end of someone else's total lack of positive regard, or any regard whatsoever, be it positive or negative. We appreciated that what people aren't aware of, they can't have any feelings toward – they can't love what they don't acknowledge. Christians understood indifference – we experienced it when we tried to tell the world they were all dying in their sin and going to burn in hell, and when they refused to come to our church or know and appreciate our Lord and Saviour. We were also well versed ourselves in demonstrating indifference toward people or issues we had no vested interest in changing or improving, or where we could effect no change favourable to our cause. We all agreed indifference had to be at the opposite end of the spectrum from love. The absence of any feeling or sentiment, empathy or interest in the other, whether feigned or inadvertent, surely had to be the opposite of what Jesus had in mind, except in the cases where one deliberately maintained one's innocence, ignorance or naivety for reasons of maintaining good mental health or physical safety. We couldn't be held responsible for loving those we went out of our way to avoid ever coming across in the first place.

Time has passed. The world is changing. Love in all its forms is needed now more than ever before. The older I get, the more I understand that the world, and by the world I mean the earth and all the people on it, has some fairly significant problems, and that I am one of them. I can tell you what I hate and what I'm afraid of, even though I know Christ teaches me to love, and tells me that love comes from God. I think about the pressing social issues in my part of the world and wonder at my own capacity for indifference when it comes to solving these issues, or even being part of the solution. I search for smiles. I stare into the blank expressions of the people around me in the street, and I think, surely, we are all as capable of love, even small expressions of it, small acts of kindness, as we are of indifference, of fear, of hate?

There is no opposite of love. There is love, and you do, or you do not. It's within us to do it, all the time, to everyone. It's how we were made. When it comes to how we were made to love, the gears work only in one direction, but at various speeds, including not at all if we so choose. They don't go backwards. There's no opposite to love. Hate, fear and indifference are different sets of gears, and let's face it, running all your gears at once is exhausting - no wonder we pick only the ones that require least resistance. Hate and fear each pull from their own momentum, but move quickly once they get going, in fact, they feed off each other. Indifference gets busy and greases those gears. But love needs someone out front to throw the propeller before it can even get off the ground. With love, you're the mechanic, the pilot the navigator and the passenger. Love is harder work, but takes you much further, and the view is better.

Why do we overcomplicate things? Does it help us in actually practicing love to think love has opposites? Or does it merely justify our own reasons for not doing it, or provide the ammunition to aim at someone else we think should be? I have been the recipient of an act of love perpetrated by someone who lacks the capacity to tie their own shoes, directed at me for no other reason than I was present in the room. It's not quantum physics. But maybe that's where we go wrong. Maybe it is. I mean, how many people in this world really *get* quantum physics? When you think about it, it apparently explains everything, but hardly anybody actually understands it.

If fear, hate and indifference figure anywhere in the love equation, it's perhaps only to demonstrate what poor excuses they make for not doing it. The propensity for fear, hate and indifference to the plight of others might not indicate so much a lack of acting upon a motivation to love, but perhaps more a sign of a lack of *being loved*. If a fearful person were properly loved, would they be so afraid? If a hateful person were properly loved, might they be less threatened by the society of others? If an indifferent person were properly loved, might they be more willing to see the world through others eyes, on purpose?

Love is not so much the opposite of fear, hate and indifference as it is the cure for it. People who are properly loved will not be afraid, hateful or naive, and it's our mission as Christians to love one another, because love comes from God. When we have learned how to be loved properly by God ourselves, through Christ, we will release love's alternatives, and seek to practice it at every opportunity. Our mission surely then as professors and Disciples of Christ is to do what He did. Love people. And do it properly.

19

How Much Abundant Life Does A Christian Really Need?

I have a new job. I am now a mental health rehabilitation support worker. You can tell I'm pretty proud. This new job entails my going out to visit people with a mental illness, usually people who have a formal diagnosis of schizophrenia. All the clients we support have been hospitalized or institutionalized at some point, usually quite recently before they sign on to our service. Our role as a support agency is to basically visit the clients in their homes and assist them in what we call ADL's – activities of daily living. This might be things like making their bed, doing the washing, cleaning the kitchen and bathroom and taking out the garbage. Disorganization can be a major problem for people with a schizophrenia diagnosis, and this can be a real problem when it comes to maintaining a tenancy, as most of the clients live in accommodation rented through a government agency. They have to stop themselves descending into squalor, or they may lose their home and be taken back to hospital. The support worker role also involves making sure the client is showering on a daily basis, exercising and eating healthy foods, and wearing clean clothes. Physical health is a major issue for people with a schizophrenia diagnosis. The anti-psychotic medication they are obliged to take has several side effects, one of which is morbid obesity. This inadvertent massive weight gain, combined with several other factors, delivers a virtual plethora of medical health issues. Aside from the schizophrenia, if you had to deal with half of what these folks have to deal with, you'd need a support worker too.

I love the job – it's different every day. The best part is hearing from the clients about their aspirations, about what they hope the future holds for them, as opposed to what others aspirations for them are. Others have lots of aspirations for them. The clinical services have them, their families have them and yes, we have them too. Some of our aspirations for them are realistic, but some sadly are not. For some reason, our unrealistic aspirations for them are called *as-yet unattained goals*. Their own unrealistic aspirations for themselves are called *delusions*.

For privacy reasons, I can't tell you very much about the clients, or divulge in any detail the things they say to me, but I can tell you that their own hopes for the future, as opposed to clinical services', center mainly around things like keeping their independence in the community and staying out of hospital, on maintaining any physical health they have, owning a pet or getting their drivers license back. Dignity. That pretty much sums up what they want. Just like a 'normal' person.

I've been wondering lately just exactly what 'normal' really is. I've concluded in my own head that society is pretty much just a silent consensus of the majority to a particular way of seeing things. It's one great, big happy, mental illness we've all agreed to live with, henceforth to be known as 'normal'. Anyone with a divergent way of thinking is seen as 'a little different', and anyone with any halfway grandiose ideas may be considered insane, or perhaps become the despotic dictator over some country somewhere.

Before I started this job, I wasn't aware for the most part of a whole sector of society living their lives in a way I might have considered to not be much of a life at all. There are people in our community, maybe living right next door to you or I, for whom getting out of bed and being able to get back into it at the end of the day will be cause of much pride and self-satisfaction today.

And here's something else I've been thinking about. The folks who are faced with the *just going to be getting out of bed and back in it today* kind of problems are something very closely resembling the folks I've thought would really benefit from church, at least as I've known it. I've been imagining that these sorts of folks were the reason for church in the first place – so that those with *less of a life* could exchange their basic, rudimentary existences for the life of the *Christian promise* – The Abundant Life. You know the one - the life of lots, the life of much, the life of many. The busy life, the full life, the blessed and bouncing, brimming-with-blessedness life. The life so full we can't help ourselves but just be bubbling up all over the place life. The life so big our arms can't hold it, and our eyes can't take it all in. The life so jam-packed with everything God has for us that we are just be run off our feet living it out. Phew, makes me tired just thinking about it.

I have believed that this is the life God wants us to have. And here we have been, chasing it all this time, wondering when it was coming, hoping it would be soon, talking to our friends about it, writing it on our prayer lists, speaking it into being, petitioning and pining away for it, longing for our Abundant life to someday arrive on our doorstep so we can start *really living,* as opposed to whatever it is we're doing now. Maybe this year! Maybe this week! Maybe today! Maybe right here in this church service! I just can't wait for my Abundant life to come! God is so good! Come, come!

Consider this.

If we, as Christians, have had the where-with-all to get up, put clean clothes on, get into our car, which we own, without help, and legally drive that car to church, and then walk upright into church, sit down unassisted, clap our two hands together in time to the music whilst appreciating the noise as being music and responding appropriately to it, if we can see the preacher from where we are sitting, hear him clearly, and understand everything he says, interacting with the folks around us without dribbling on them or punching them in the face, and after all this get up and go home to our house.....perhaps, just perhaps, we are a little bit more "abundant" than we might have thought?

I went to church last Sunday morning, and, as usual, I saw a lot of very happy people. We were all dressed nicely, everyone was freshly bathed and all of us were on our best behavior. No one swore or hit anyone else. No one got sick on the back of the person in front of them. No one came in naked, and no one went up to anyone else to ask for food or a smoke. No one had to be carried in. No one fitted or had to be taken to hospital. No one had been in an earthquake or a flood or had their house burn down since we last saw them. And despite all this, we all stood up at the end and asked God to bless us. We, who are so blessed, asked God for *more of the same, thank you very much.*

So where were the ones with the dirty clothes, the unwashed, the ones who hadn't had their breakfast? Where were the hitters and the spitters, the sick and the infirm, the ones with no driver's license, no car and no money for a bus ticket? Where were the ones who just had their anti-psychotic medication yesterday, or their chemotherapy last Tuesday? Where were the ones who didn't remember they had a washing machine to do their laundry in, and who wore the same underwear all week? Where were the earthquake survivors, the flood victims and the homeless? Maybe they were there with us, but if they were, they were very well disguised as something else.

As us.

If we have the means, and the capacity, to get ourselves along to church in the first place, then just maybe church is not meant for the likes of us. Maybe church isn't meant for people who are abundant already. Maybe we ought to get out and make some room. Come to think of it, most of the Christians I know probably don't need any more abundance. After all, how much abundance does one Christian actually need?

I think we in this self-obsessed, materialistic society have become so accustomed to believing we are in lack, always praying and petitioning for more than we already have now, that we fail to perceive our own present state of abject prosperity. We *are* blessed, people. Not only do we live under the grace of God, we also have financial, psychosocial and material abundance far above the realistic aspirations of most of the rest of the world, and probably beyond many in our own communities. What is it that we hope church, and God, and Christianity, will do for us, more than what we already have and are?

Perhaps we could draw on both our church, and our faith, more deeply to help us become 1) grateful and then 2) content. Oh, and maybe even 3) aware of and interested in facilitating blessing and abundance for others who perhaps aren't quite as blessed and abundant as we already are. I believe that individuals possessed by, and a movement made up of, people in possession of these three particular qualities could be considered abundant indeed. How much abundance does a Christian actually need? Enough to become inspired, and mobilized, to facilitate abundance for others, in ways that matter. And not just for eternity. For the here, and for the now.

20

The Poor You Will Always Have With You

When he was here on earth, my friend Jesus - bless Him - had this habit of eating out and drinking with certain types of people it was considered inappropriate for him to be seen with. It annoyed people, mostly his inner circle of friends, and they sometimes told him how annoyed they were about it. No, not only did the weirdo's have Jesus over to their houses for dinner, they gave him presents. Expensive presents. Once, Jesus had a woman smother his head with expensive perfume while he ate dinner at a leper's house. To the disciples of Jesus, this was a disgusting exhibition. Rather than enjoy seeing their teacher being gifted with an anointing by a generous worshipper, Jesus' friends got well and truly ticked off. Maybe it was because it had never occurred to them to do what she did. Maybe they felt this woman was moving in on their turf, or just making a spectacle of herself. Maybe they thought she was attention seeking, or even trying to seduce Jesus. Who knows what they thought. All we know is what they said.

"What a *waste*."

The Son of God, the Way, Truth and Life, reclines beside them at the table within an arms length, words of wisdom dripping from his tongue, grace exuding from his every pore, and these, his friends and followers, consider a simple yet significant act of sacrifice and kindness extended toward him to be *a waste*?

*****

I once had a conversation with the pastor of a church I was attending about the possibility of starting up a welfare program for the poor in our community. He suggested I not go to the trouble. As far as he was concerned, our community had no poor. There is no poverty in this city, he said, and with that, succinctly and effectively absolved himself of losing any sleep, or any of his churches resources, for their sakes.

*****

Jesus looked up from the table to where his disciples stood grumbling, the fragrant oil still dripping down his forehead, the woman's hands still in his hair, and answered their mutterings without disdain or anger. He knew they were, at least in that moment, lacking in any genuine concern for the poor. Their complaints against the gift had sprung more from their own shame and embarrassment than from a sense of duty or charity. Casting aspersions on the woman's act was the only way to mask their own failure to honour their master properly. Rather than rebuke them outright, Jesus chose to honour the woman and her act, whilst gently prompting the conscience of his disciples.

"The poor", he says, "you will always have with you. But you will not always have me."

I'm going soon. Time is short. She is preparing me properly for my death. Relax; I'm not angry with you.

But think about what I've said. Yes, this perfume could have been sold and the money given to the poor. So, when I am gone, do what your conscience just told you was right. And for as long as you have the poor with you, do what is right. And...you will always have the poor with you.

The poor.

Always.

With you.

*****

Having been a church-going Christian most of my life, I appreciate that mission work is an important part of what Church is, and what it does and is seen to be doing. But it's not just brown-skinned, big-eyed babies with distended bellies and bare-feet that qualifies as our poor. I know we don't like to hear it, but many of our poor live between brick walls and own televisions.

Everywhere I went for months after my conversation with the pastor, I looked at people in our town differently. There are no poor here, I told myself, more to justify my doing nothing for them, and my not planning to any time soon, than anything else. Not poor, not poor, not poor. It became easier to think of them as just plain old lazy for not fulfilling my aspirations for them, than to consider myself lazy for not doing anything to help them meet the ones they had for themselves.

****

If there are no poor with you, you haven't been listening. Jesus never said anything about the great paying job we would always have with us, or the two-story rendered brick four-bedder we would always have with us. He didn't even say anything about the husband or wife we would always have with us, the friends, the church, or the pile of money we have in the bank we would always have with us. The poor. They are what Jesus said we would always have with us. Strange. Where do you suppose they could've gotten to?

*****

Ever wondered what it must have felt like for that woman, hearing the disciples' snarky remarks about her obviously well thought out (but quite risky) gesture? What if Jesus had pushed her away? What if that perfume was the last thing on earth *she* actually owned? What if she were supposed to save that perfume for her parents' funeral, or for her own? What if she were actually *one of the poor* the disciples were referring to? Nice, you guys. *Real* tactful.

*****

The poor are with us. And there are more ways to be poor than just financial. Whatever your currency is, that's how you judge worth. For some it's fiscal, for others, it's relational, others, political. Jesus didn't care as much for the monetary price of the woman's gift as he did for it's spiritual worth. He saw a woman who possessed what we might call these days 'emotional intelligence'. As far as Jesus was concerned, she *got it*. And he bought into that currency. The disciples' whining was a ruse, and Jesus knew it. Buy in, he said. I have come not for the *things* you will always have with you, but for the ones you will always have with you.

And so, my friends have you and I.

21

The Theology Of Evacuation

Lots of talk about heaven and hell and the end of the world being bantered about lately. I've had several conversations myself with people just in the last week on the subject, and the release of Rob Bells new book (Love Wins) seems somewhat timely also, but more about that later. Concerns about how much time humanity may have left underpin most of the conversations between Christians on social networking sites also. Unarticulated, yet mutually understood. Pray, they all say, which is what we do when we don't know what else to do. I wonder - if the world is ending and Judgment Day is upon us, what exactly are we Christians praying for?

For three days this week I was in Sydney for some work related training, and whilst staying at the Holiday Inn I had the pleasure of breakfasting beside a group of very well groomed American gentlemen, all wearing t-shirts cheerily stating the world is ending on the 21st May this year. A happy start to he day. On further investigation, I found that the group are part of a worldwide push by an organisation called Family Radio, affiliated with a man called Harold Camping*. Family Radio are sending groups all over the world to inform the unaffiliated of the - er - good news, which is, of course, Family Radio get to go to heaven when the world end in a couple of weeks, and everyone else is in big trouble. How abjectly considerate of them.

Yes, it seems that the end of the world is coming...again. For anyone who has been involved in Christianity in its various forms for any period of time in the past 50 years or so, we have heard it all before. Mind you, world events of late have had me back with my head in the Bible, poring over Matthew 24. It does sound somewhat familiar, more so than ever before - wars, rumours of wars, earthquakes, floods and famines. Very big moons = signs in the heavens. Scary stuff.

Earlier this month, Rob Bell spoke at the New York Ethical Culture Society about his new book Love Wins; A Book About Heaven, Hell, and the Fate of Every Person Who Ever Lived. The book has been widely criticized in the media for months, despite the fact it was only released a couple of days ago. I've been observing the debate closely - I enjoy Bell's contributions to the emergent theological discussion very much, and appreciate the conversations that inevitably spring from them. I know Bell expects criticism, he says so, and isn't surprised by it. However, I am sure he is surprised by how many times theologians threaten to dismiss him as a heretic. I wonder if they have considered how absurd this is, considering

Bell insists he is not a theologian.

Anyway, I was reading the transcript of his presentation in New York and in part of it Bell discusses how he is interested in challenging traditional notions of heaven and hell. This is especially relevant at the moment, considering the conversations that we're having about what the end of the world means for us. By us, I mean all of us, not just Christians. The Christianity I have practiced for twenty-nine years dictates that Jesus Christ is coming back to earth, in the clouds, and when He does, everyone on earth will recognize that it's Him, even those who say they don't believe in Him. Then, He will take all the Christians up to heaven with Him and leave everyone else behind. What happens to the ones left behind varies depending on exactly whom you talk to. In fact, who gets to go with Him also varies depending on exactly who you talk to. And a lot of what Christianity consists of is basically self-adjustment to whatever idea you have of who gets to go to heaven when Jesus comes back. A Christian might reinvent themselves in relation to their view of the end-times many times over the course of a few years, depending on whose teaching they are currently subscribed to. The problem is, despite the confidence of some, no one really knows who gets to go, and we know that we don't know. This insecurity about getting to go when Jesus comes back runs so deep that when someone comes along who acts like they don't know just a little bit less than others about who gets to go and who doesn't, we take that to mean they might actually know a little bit more. So people like David Koresh and Harold Camping begin their illustrious careers. Even more scary stuff.

Now, I'm no theologian. Just in case you missed that, I'll say it again. I am not a theologian. I have studied theology, and have a Bible College qualification, but for me, none of what Christianity espouses or embodies matters unless it has a practical application for people in their lives. I don't believe Christianity should be merely an academic pursuit. What mattered to Jesus was people, and that's good enough for me. Now, Jesus is coming back again, I believe that. But what that means for us, all of us, I actually don't know. I've reinvented enough times in my own life to appreciate that I have pretty much swayed toward whatever way of thinking and being that is most conducive to my own ass-saving. The thing is, and I do feel a bit sad saying this, but you don't actually have to look very deep to understand the over-arching Christian theology of end times. The way Christians behave much of the time now is the way we will behave when the crunch comes. Sad, but true.

Bell, in the New York interview, touches on something else, something I believe Christians should find disturbing, and it isn't anything to do with arguments that Bell is a Universalist. Although he is specifically referring

140

to concepts of heaven and hell, Bell alludes to the idea that end times are a theology of evacuation.

Evacuation. How different this reads from the traditional party line concerning the rapture, which basically says, "We (Christians) are good - everyone else is bad. We deserve to go, they don't. It's sad, but fair. Now, bring it on." Rapture implies something very right, good and just. It will be comfortable, convenient and timely. However, evacuation implies removal from the region of the disaster to another place, whilst the disaster goes on being disastrous. It implies impending doom, urgency, *emergency*. It implies not just departing, but also a leaving behind. *Leaving behind.* What, or whom, will we be leaving behind? Do we, dare I say it, *care*? Does that sound like something you feel comfortable with?

I made a wry remark to my friend on the last morning we breakfasted while the t-shirt men sat huddled at the next table. I noticed they were all well-dressed, and from another English-speaking country. They appeared well-resourced, and healthy. I presume they viewed themselves as missionaries to our fine land. I wondered how much money they had spent getting themselves to Australia and putting themselves up in the Holiday Inn so that they could spread their apocalyptic message to our unwashed masses. I remarked to my friend, as I pointed to the newspaper headline about Japan, that a place like that could really use a few fit, well-intentioned and well-resourced men right about now. Or, if their tickets to Australia were non-refundable, how many communities a thousand kilometres or so north of us in Queensland still needed some cleaning up after the worst floods in a century. Or how New Zealand has been crying out for chaplains in the wake of their recent earthquakes. Now, I know I didn't go to any of those places either, but given the opportunity and the resources to do so, I would have. To be perfectly frank, I drew conclusions concerning how these particular Christians chose to act out their faith that week. And it made me taste a little bit of my breakfast twice.

I say all of that, to say this. Christian end-times teaching is pretty much a theology of evacuation. I have observed that when Christians begin to discuss Jesus' return, the conversation begins to break into bipolarities. Us and them. Go and stay. Righteous and unrighteous. Heaven and hell. Saved and un-saved. The discomfort we feel at the prospect of the 'end of the world' seems largely limited to how we personally will be affected. Will I be ready? Will my family know Christ in time? Will He find me about His business? Will I be one of the elect? I wonder if any Christian's thoughts ever project beyond the actual event? Have we ever considered what will the world be like when all the Christians leave? What will happen to the cancer patients, the abuse victims, the poverty stricken, the disabled and impaired?

It's actually a very disturbing question for a Christian to ask themselves. What distresses me more than thinking I might not go with Jesus is the thought that when I do, perhaps no one would even notice. Sometimes I think the world will be pleased to just have us out of the way, for the fat lot of good we do a lot of the time. I have considered that despite the importance we believe we have in the scheme of things, Christians may turn out to be like an annoying, bossy aunt who dithers around the place thinking she's indispensable to everyone, then makes a huge production out of leaving to go on a more important mission. When she's been gone ten minutes, everyone forgets she was ever there. In fact the place is a lot quieter, and everyone gets on better without her. Now wouldn't that be something.

The thing is, the more I think about it, the more reticent I am to go. With Jesus, that is. I am wondering if He would mind terribly if I stayed behind. Perhaps I have an inflated sense of my own capacity, or a diminished sense of what the world will be like when Jesus takes all the Christians, but it sounds like something I'd be interested in being a part of. The world, after all, will still have cancer patients, the abused, poverty and need and crisis. I know I'm supposed to be looking forward to going to Heaven and getting my Reward and all that, but I'm actually a bit concerned with what the world will be like. I am thinking of putting in for a...what do you call the opposite of a transfer? I don't want to be evacuated. I want to stay. I want in.

I reiterate my belief that there are no others, there is only us. If thinking of Jesus' coming back actually makes me more self-centred, more self-righteous and more self-interested, then for me, the second coming itself is anti-Christ. When I see the disasters on TV, I don't actually think of my own exit plan; all I see are people. Lost, hurting, confused, terrified people. Now, I know when my child, my friend or my neighbour is feeling all of those things, what they want to hear the most is my assurance that I am here, I will never leave them, no matter what I'll be helping them...they are not alone. I know it's not proper to say so, but I'm having some real problems with this whole too-bad-so-sad, end-times, rapture, Jesus coming back and taking us all away thing. If Jesus were already here now, would He go?

22

Why I Don't Go To Women's Conferences,

And My Own Personal String Theory

I don't go to many Christian conferences these days. Well, I'm lying about that. I actually don't go to *any* Christian conferences. I especially don't go to the conferences I'm expected to go to. You know the ones. *You know*. Don't make me say it. I'll spell it out for you. I'm a woman. I'm a Christian. Yes – *those* conferences.

Christian women's conferences.

I used to go, and I used to enjoy them. They were certainly a lot of fun, and I'm sure they still are, but I don't want to go to any more. I probably kept attending women's conferences for about two years longer than I should have. Then something happened. I couldn't work out why about a week before the big date, along with my last registration installment, I would come out in a nervous rash. It's stupid, I know. I've sung on stage at these functions. I've even been the *speaker* at several of these things over the years. But now whenever I think about them, I feel the need to visit my doctor for a prescription for Valium.

I thought for a while it was just my agoraphobia playing up – I feel the same way about movie theaters these days. I almost had to be sedated when my family and I went to see Avatar on Boxing Day a couple of years ago. But there's something else about women's conferences. It's not just the crowds, the noise and the unallocated seating that brings me out in a sweat. I think I've worked it out: it's the distinct lack of *men*.

Large groups of just women – and Christian women particularly – make me very, very nervous. It could be just me, but it feels like there's just way too much intuition in the room. You can never know what two, let alone two thousand, Spirit-filled women in a room might do. Literally. You also never know what they might say. They seldom stick to the script, the notes, or the program, even if the script, the notes and the program are their own creation. Women at a women's conference love an itinerary. It makes great confetti.

Men just bring a certain something to a gathering. I know that sometimes it is just poor taste in shirts and unusual smells, but there's something else as well. They bring *the ground*. In the cacophony of a collective estrogen-fueled God-adoration session, complete with swaying arms and glistening eyes, there's nothing that can bring a girl back to reality like the gentle, earthy snore of her husband in the seat beside her. A man's musky scent and squirming hips are enough to snap us out of any wandering, super-spiritual tangent we may have allowed ourselves to drift off on during a particularly inspiring sermon.

The presence of men serves to remind women that the world and everything in it is really all made of dirt. This is as it should be. If we had our way, everything would be shiny or sparkly, there would be no fat or hair anywhere, and all creation would vibrate at a level sounding eerily like James Blunt.

God likes men, and so do I. I like their humor. God made them funny looking too, which is always super. I also like the way men think; straight up and down – in levels, zones and in boxes. Women think like tangled string. I think like tangled string. My string needs to go in a box, onto a level, then be in a zone. That's why I keep men handy at all times. I married one, gave birth to three and whenever they aren't available, I go out into the street and fix my eyes on one, just to reassure myself all is right with the world; I will not be consumed by my string, today.

I think that whenever too many women get together in one place and let loose with all their string, it's the most terrifying thing in the universe. Not self-organizing, like, it could be argued, creation, but more like chaos, or the worst kind of entropy. At women's conferences, I feel like disarray is taking me over from all directions. I feel as though in amongst all that emotion and thinking and noise and string all I can know for certain is that at some point someone will want the building back, and we will have to go. And I feel happy only because of that certainty. You see now why I don't find it a pleasurable experience.

So please don't take it personally when I don't accept your very tempting invitation to a Christian women's conference. They look great, really they do. It not you, it's absolutely me. And I'm okay with it. While you're all in conference mode, comparing your string, working out how to enhance your string, making your string into pretty shapes and thinking of ways to color and kink and primp your string, I'll just stay home with my grunting, snoring, smelly, pragmatist with the bad shirt. The one who likes string. The one who is mystified, thrilled and excited by string. The one who can't get enough of me and my string, and likes me to wrap him in string and drag him around the house…sorry, that's probably enough of that. You all go right ahead now and have yourselves a good time. ☺

23

Linda

For my friend Linda,*** who has a schizophrenia diagnosis, and is the most holy person I think I've ever met.

Ragged and elegant

Fragile as cigarette ash

You collect all the pieces

Before you open your door

Your skin like dust

Your lips swollen

Your mouth kissed by the gods

Just left through the open window

Lying under your bed

Holding their breath

Licking you from their palms

Waiting in your nest until I'm gone

Painted mermaids, four pears

Piece of a sacred tree

Some of the sea

Sister with the tired eyes

And you, with your long hair

Seeing the future

Born again as your mothers mother

With all her seed and blood and fear

Held like heaven in the air

You are holy, holy

And god is everywhere.

24

If Bad Mothers Don't Buy Their Kids School Photos,

Then I'm A Bad Mother

I'm writing this post in the hope it will "out" what I suspect is a huge secret movement amongst the mothers of the school-aged children of this world. Or not. Maybe I really am the worst mother in the world. You see - I don't buy school photos. Haven't for years. I simply won't believe I'm alone in this. Now is your time to 'fess up. If you haven't refused outright to pay someone good money you worked to get for hideous photographs of your babies, then you must have at least balked once or twice. Or is that just me?

We have four children, now aged 23, 18, 16 and 11. Over the years, we spent probably hundreds of dollars on school photos. And where are they now? In a box, under the house. The subjects of the world's most expensive mug shots flatly refuse to allow us to display them publicly. And I don't blame them. Those photos are in no way true representations of the wonderful humans they claim to depict. Hair that I know is blonde looks like the colour of muddy creek water. Eyes I fully know sparkle with mischief and good health appear as heavy lidded and bloodshot as those of a world-weary, middle-aged crack addict. Cheery smiles become goofy

 grimaces. I have photos of my children tantrumming at birthday parties and lying in hospital beds with broken limbs that contain more joy per pixel than those dreadful, pretend happy snaps. The only one laughing is the photographer. He has my money, and he knows I worked harder for it than he bloody-well did.

I have managed to actually frame for display in my home only four of the eighty so or pictures that have been taken of our children at school, but I've had to mount them behind bulletproof glass and rivet the frames with titanium before screwing them to the wall. My offspring despise these portraits with a passion usually reserved for my attempts to woot-woot for them at school presentations and concerts, or kiss them when I drop them off. But that's another story. I can understand their disdain for the school photos, really I can. See the year nine school photograph of me above for point in case. Would you want to remember yourself that way? Nobody likes to look at a photo of themselves taken at a time when their mother cut their hair, forced them to dress in horrid clothes, when they followed ridiculous trends in jewelry and were dealing with various facial dermatological issues.

Not having to worry about the financial and emotional blackmail that is school photography is one of the best things about homeschooling. We taught our children at home for four years. We don't keep the photos we took of our four children over those four years in a box under the house, I can tell you now.

It's not just the fact that school photos are obnoxiously facile; it's the fact that they are obscenely expensive. The latest envelope to come home this week has offered me a basic pack for twenty-nine dollars, consisting of a class photo, and four small portraits measuring about two inches by three and a half inches each. The packs increase in price and content incrementally from there, up to about fifty dollars. And I only have one child in school. Why do they cost so much? I can get a reprint of the best photo ever taken of my child in his whole life from a photo-printing kiosk for about sixty cents, whilst a "premium" pack of these terrible school snapshots of my child could quite possibly set me back the cost of a small camera. You add it up - three hundred students, at thirty dollars a pop, for one days "work". I think this is why you never hear someone at a party tell you "I'm a school photographer." They only spend twenty one days a year in this country, travelling from campus to campus photographing three hundred students a day, before heading off abroad to slum it the other forty nine weeks of the year in opulent villas in Tuscany or France.

I especially hate those hideous group/class photos. Not only does your own child look like he's been sleeping outdoors in a bus shelter for a week after being mussed up by an unruly crowd before having a sandwich smeared across his face, but so does everyone else's. Class photos also do not bring out the best in parents. Thanks to the class photo, you and every other parent may now freely cast aspersions on the other members of your child's class in the privacy of your own home, and make derogatory presumptions concerning their family, without ever having to meet them in the flesh and realise how nice they truly are. I don't like the way class photos make me behave. *There are seriously too many freckles on that face, don't they know about sunscreen? Get a load of that dental work, or lack of it. I see the bowl haircut is still de rigueur.* Argh! I hate myself. Even more than I don't want to judge other parents based on what their child looks like, I don't want that done to me. I struggle just keeping my eyes straight ahead at traffic lights. A class photo would provide too much fodder for my critical side. Get thee behind me, Nikon.

I know there is a huge controversy these days about digitally re-touching school photos. While as a parent I personally abhor the practice (tiger-parent, face it now, or face it later, your child simply isn't and never will be perfect) as a pre-teen, I would have given anything for a way to make my photo into the Dolly Cover Girl competition entry everyone seemed to expect from me. When I was twelve, a boy from another school who liked me asked me for a photo of myself, so I gave him one of those wallet-sized jobs from my school photos from the year before. It was the only picture I had of myself, other than a couple of blurry Polaroid instamatics taken on our Christmas holidays of me in a terry toweling jumpsuit standing next to my two brothers taken at the Pet Porpoise Pool. On receipt of the photo, the boy sent a message through a friend from his footy team to my friend in the netball team that I was dropped. I don't blame him. That photo were *ugh-leeh*.

So come on, fess up. You've considered rebelling and not sending that envelope back to school, haven't you? Whilst I in no way advocate the collective putting-out-of-business of a whole industry of school photographers, I would propose we lobby for them to at least give us our monies worth. Surely they could take along a hairdresser to primp our progeny's locks, particularly the male ones? Maybe they could set up a little powder room where a make-up person might administer some minor ablutions in order to remove all traces of foodstuffs, dried bodily secretions and incorrectly toned acne cream? For the money, I really don't think this is too much to ask. As for me, I won't be buying those blasted photos this year, or any other year. I'll use that money to keep paying off their very expensive education. It's funny how, just like the school photos, they haven't thanked me for that either. Oh well, at least I'll have nothing to remember it by.

25

Jesus Is For Losers

Jesus is for losers.

Jesus is not for winners. If you're a winner, Jesus is not for you. You see, Jesus saves. Winners don't need saving, except perhaps from their addiction to competition. People who see others as competitors are nothing like Christ. Christ saw people, just *saw them*. And being *truly seen* was enough to change them. No, people who need to win don't need Jesus to do it. Jesus is not for them.

Jesus isn't for the ones at the top. Jesus knows nothing about it; you see, Jesus Himself never went to the top. Oh, they tried to make him their leader, their messiah, even their king, but He wouldn't have it. He kept slipping away and going back to hang out with the ones that those at the top considered to be at the bottom. The ones at the top hated Him for that. And it just confirmed once and for all that He wasn't for them. The ones at the top always want Jesus to be their leader so they can claim His name and have their agenda cleaned up by association. But Jesus doesn't mingle with those who see themselves as leaders amongst men. He lives, eats and dies amongst the merest of men, and funnily enough, men follow Him because of it.

Jesus isn't for the go-getters. Go getters get going way past the types Jesus hangs with. Go getters don't need Jesus for anything - they just go get it for themselves.

Jesus is not for the self-sufficient. Jesus is for the ones who need miracles. Jesus makes everyday things into answers for everyday needs - pennies from fishes mouths pay taxes, mud makes a poultice for blind eyes, pots of water appease wedding guests, a boys lunch feeds a thousand hungry stomachs. The self-sufficient solve such earthy problems out for themselves.

No, Jesus is not for the furnished, the fixed-up or the famous. He's for the fallible and the faulty, the fallen and the flawed. Jesus is for the filthy, the fouled, and the foundling. Orphans and outcasts are His children. The poor, in pocket and in spirit, are Jesus friends. The Jesus they love is the true saviour, for it is such men that require the kind of salvation Jesus offers.

While ever there are those in the world who feel they must lord over, profit from and win against others, the Jesus who saves will always make His home with servants, slaves and with losers.

For the poor, things can only ever get better. Blessed are they, Jesus says, for they don't just get something better, they get the whole Kingdom.

Jesus is for losers.

26

Eight Pieces Of Advice On Marriage

It's twenty-three years now I've been married. I've ever done anything else as long as I've done this. I did take a year off however, in two parts. We separated twice, for about half a year each time, so I count that as a year off. As it turns out, I've been married most of my life, and I'm only forty-three. That's something to brag about right there, I don't care who you are.

Sometimes in a marriage, things get tough. Ours has certainly been difficult at times. We've had fights. Nobody won, by the way. But it's been great too. There are a whole lot of people giving advice out there on marriage, and I'm about to be one of them. Here's some of what I think I know. Be warned; it's brutally honest. It might scare you off marriage if you're considering it, but you know what? If this lot scares you, you're probably not quite as ready to get married as you think you are.

Eight pieces of advice on marriage:

1) People yell when they're scared.

If the person you married is yelling, you can bet they're scared. Maybe not of you, but they're frightened of something. And if you're the one doing

160

the yelling, you need to stop and ask what it is you're afraid of right now. Stop yelling, and go away and work it out, then come back and finish what you were going to say, if it still matters. It probably won't. The best way not to yell at each other when you're married is to always see the person who is talking to you as someone who was not put on this earth to make you happy, is not the cause of your unhappiness, who does not owe you anything, and who is nothing like you. This will change everything.

(Now, some people yell and hit at the same time. This still means they're scared, but hitting makes them feel bigger and stronger. If you are married to someone who yells and hits, you don't need to stay around to find out what they're scared of. Once hitting starts, all deals are off. Hitting is never, ever okay.)

2) Self-sacrifice does not add up somewhere as brownie points, incrementally.

The only thing martyrdom and marrying should ever have in common is a few consonants and one vowel. If you want to give up that thing you love to do for your partner, like dancing, singing, art, going to the opera, belly dancing or university for example, and they haven't asked you to, then I would say don't give it up. They won't thank you, they won't be grateful, and odds are they won't even notice. If they don't mention it, keep on doing it and don't stop unless you want to. If they do ask you to give up something that you love simply because it inconveniences them, makes them feel threatened or makes them look like they actually haven't got a life of their own, tell them to get a life, and ask them if the thing you love you have to give up can be them.

However, if you happen to love porn, or adultery, and the person you are married to asks you to give it up, I would say do so. Or they may yell at you. See 1) for more on this.

3) Children are not an answer. They are another question.

This is a nice way of saying children are not a solution, they are another problem. Now, it's true we never solve all our problems: we only ever exchange them for other problems we are prepared to live with. Before you have children, if it can be arranged try to make sure you both have a manageable set of problems, because the baby will bring some problems it will expect you to manage as well as the ones you already have. And babies selfishly refuse to become involved in solving your problems. The other reason you want to have a manageable set of problems between you when you begin raising a child is because those problems you do have will undoubtedly come out in any therapy your child has at any point in their life. Another reason to investigate possible causes for 1).

4) Men think in levels. Women think in string.

This is not open for discussion. This is the way things are. This also applies to people of the same gender in relationships. Two women = string + string. In this case, get your string working in harmony. Knit. Macrame. Crochet. No lynching, garroting or other jute-inspired acts of emotional violence. Two men = levels + levels. Be like two elevators working in synchronicity. A man and a woman = string + level. String goes on a level. That's how it works. The brains are different. String cannot be made to act like a level. Levels are too rigid to behave like string. Just accept it. Life is too short, believe me.

5) Gender assignment when it comes to household tasks is so passé, darling.

About 98% percent of the arguments you will have in the lifetime of your marriage will be about this.

All you need to clean a toilet properly is a good sturdy brush, disinfectant and about five energetic minutes. You don't need to have breasts, or a uterus. Anyone can do it. It may also be found to be possible to be in possession of testicles, *and* enough manual dexterity to place clothes in a washing machine. People who marry without ever discussing who did the housework in their home of origin are setting themselves up for the worst, and probably the most consistent, set of conflicts they will ever have. Arguments about money and sex come and go, as do money and sex, but someone will always need to clean the shower. The best way to resolve arguments about housework is for both parties to make a deal that no one gets invited to do housework if it is convenient for them. We all do it. No one also gets rewarded or even congratulated for doing things that sustain the basics of life for everyone. If you're not prepared to make this type of bargain, strap on an apron, sugar, it's your turn to cook...*again*.

6) Your bodies are for each other's pleasure, entertainment and amusement.

Just have fun with one another. Don't critique your partner's body. Naked bodies are lovely things, no matter whether fat or thin, young or old. It's a given that men's bodies are funnier looking than women's, so giggling is permitted in these cases, but snarky comments are not for either party. It will matter less and less as the years go by whether the body you enjoy is toned, tanned, trim and taut and begin to matter more whether that body is familiar and friendly. There is something very comforting as you grow older about holding close a naked, very familiar body.

7) You won't go to hell if you get divorced.

If you've come to the point of even entertaining a divorce, then you have probably already endured one version of hell. Who's to say who is wrong and who is right? There comes a point when it doesn't matter any more. Hopefully, that point is before you decide the person you once loved more than life itself has committed such horrible acts of vitriol against you there is no possibility of reconciliation, and little probability of forgiveness. Get over it now, get over it later: sooner or later, the result is the same. If it truly is over, get yourself over it, the sooner the better, and get on with your life.

8) Having sex before you get married is not the worst sin you can commit against yourself or someone else.

People sometimes marry very young because they think they might go to hell for having sex before marriage. But I think the hell they are afraid of going to is sometimes nothing compared to the hell two adolescents can perpetrate on each other in practicing their childish, self-centred immaturity, all from within the sanctity of marriage. I'm not advocating sex before marriage. I am advocating not getting married for the purpose of simply eliminating any need for self-control. It's a lot easier to stop yourself from having sex with someone you have grown to love than it is to stop yourself from leaving someone you have grown to despise. Believe me.

Well, those are the most important ones, at least, the most important that occur to me right now. Oh, and another thing – relax. Your partner won't change as much as you hope, but they will delight you in ways you could never expect. Hang in there if you can – I did, and I don't regret a thing, but we had two willing parties. Marriage itself is great, but can never be greater than the two people involved in it. Work on yourself, invest in yourself and in each other, build each other up, forgive, bend sometimes, let the small stuff go, stand up for what you believe, don't give away the things which you know to be truly who you are, and don't expect the other person to give away the things that make them truly who they are. See them as God does as often as you're able, with compassion and patience, and hope for their future, because it's yours too. Love them with grace, and gentleness and kindness, sometimes forgotten between married people. And nurture that thing between you that will stay alive and keep you connected when your bodies grow old and tired.

May God bless your marriage, as ours is blessed.

27

Further Advice On Marriage - You Can't Change Someone Else

Due to the huge popularity of my last post Eight Pieces Of Advice on Marriage, I have decided to pen a few extra tips. By the way, did you know if you take the "i" out of married, you get marred? Maybe...on the other hand, I don't think that actually works. Forget it.

Todays piece of advice is - forget trying to change your partner. This is because it won't work. The truth is if your partner changes and it happens to be something you wanted them to change, it's a happy coincidence. Despite what you may think, their changing is not evidence of their love for you, nor their willingness to sacrifice themselves for the greater good i.e.: what you want. It's not that you're not a terrific person, you're great...but not that great. Let me put it this way - ever heard the saying "Any club that would have me as a member, I wouldn't want to join"? Well, anyone who changes - and by change, I mean things like gives something up they like, takes something on they don't like, adapts their beliefs, compromises their morals, tweaks their personal ethics, surrenders their faith, adjusts their personality, that sort of thing, just because you asked them to is not someone you would want as a partner. A person who is prepared to compromise who and what they intrinsically are to please someone else at best needs counseling, at worst, a high-level job in advertising.

Single people, particularly the youngish ones, think when they get married they'll spend a lot of time having a) their needs met, b) splendid, guilt-free sex and c) their partner still be as interested in pleasing them as they were when they were dating. The truth is that when you're married you spend a lot of time learning to become the sort of person you probably thought you were marrying, i.e.: patient, content, loving, sweet, considerate, accepting, forgiving, gracious, kind, and thoughtful. Notice the big differences there? Marriage fantasy = **having**. Marriage reality = **learning**. As they say in the movies, you'd better listen to me *if you want to live.*

I suggest that if you are looking for a long term relationship with someone that is interested primarily in meeting all your needs for the whole duration of your time together, who brings you a coffee or beer or tea whenever you need a little pick up, who always tells you that you look fantastic, who will maintain very low expectations of you and who will accept your whims and make them their priority without question, well, this is actually the exact job description of a hairdresser.

A little story. When I was about 18, there was this guy who wanted to date me. He was older than me, a little creepy but generally nice, and he was a

Christian, so that was two things right there he had over everyone else I'd dated up to then. Around the time he was trying to convince me to go out with him, he sold his car and bought another one. I remember him complaining after he brought it back from the lot, "It feels nothing like my old one to drive, the clutch is really stiff, and I can't find the gears. I think what I need to do is take it out for a long, hard thrash. Once I've driven it as hard as I can, it'll come around to my way of driving." Even as an 18 year old woman, I knew enough about cars to appreciate that thinking you can change a car by driving it in a particular way was a little weird, let alone improbable. Nevertheless, my potential suitor took his new-used car out for a couple of hours and drove it as just rough as he could. He crashed the gears up and down and pounded the clutch pedal as hard as possible to the floor. On returning, he confirmed with great satisfaction, "Yep, it's great now. It's just the way I like it." Oblivious to the bemused expressions of our group, he remained absolutely convinced it was his power over, and rough handling of, his new car, and not his way of driving it, that had changed over the past few hours. I might have been young and immature, but I knew at that moment this was not a guy I wanted to be in any kind of relationship with.

In my experience of marriage, much of it comes down to negotiation. I'll give you an example. A while ago, Ben promised to never lie to me about his smoking and drinking. Prior to that, I'd tried for a long time to get him to stop smoking and drinking, but that hadn't worked, because his smoking and drinking has been part of a deeper problem that needed addressing. I realised *eventually* I couldn't make him stop - he needed to find a reason to do so for himself - and my insistence he change for me only made him become a super-proficient sneak and liar, causing a huge rift between us. In the end, I had to let go of my need for Ben to change, even though it would have done him physical good, especially if it were *for me.* I had to accept he might smoke and drink forever, and make my own choice based on that. Eventually, Ben had to stop smoking and drinking when the consequences of both became impossible for him to bear, and it was made easier for him to do so when I let go of my expectation that he do it for my sake. We have a pact now; he is free to smoke and drink, but he cannot lie to me about it. That way, he always has the freedom to choose, and I always have the right to know exactly what is going on. This works, because the lies and the sneaking around and the deception and the mistrust did more damage to our marriage than the smoking and drinking ever did.

Trust me on this one - you can't change the person you're married to. Nor would you want to. No, *really*. My advice? Having a partner is like buying curtains. Good ones will service your requirements for a very long time, so never choose based on your current tastes or the present trends. Find out what makes them operate, and make sure they function well without you needing to call up for instructions way before you get them home. Don't just grab whatever is available, thinking you can worry about it later. Plan on having them for a while, and take your time choosing. Finally, just remember that once you've committed, it's going to take a lot of trouble to start again, so always go for whatever you just can't imagine living without. You can always paint your walls a different colour, in fact, you probably will. The moral of this story? In marriage relationships, as with the purchase of major home furnishings, change is inevitable. Just be sure and presume it will always be *you* doing the changing.

28

The Burning Bush Beside The Bed,

And Other Things You Need To Know About Men

I have been observing a particular phenomenon for many years now, and, after careful study and observation, I am now ready to publish my findings.

Domestically, politically, religiously and socially, the gap continues to close between traditional male and female gender disparities (and rightly so). Even so, there do still exist some places where God meets men exclusively, under conditions such that women can neither conceive of, nor appreciate, the nature of their coalition. One place I've observed one such peculiar union occur is so unusual, it surpasses the burning bush of Moses and the speaking ass of Balaam. The sacred nature of this holy place is so bizarre as to be bathed in sublime mystery, yet so domestic as to be almost laughable.

If you're a man, you have such a portal to heaven available to you right now, perhaps very close by, and maybe you're not even aware of it. You might be utilising it as you read this and not even realise it. If you're a woman, and you have a man about the place, I think you'd best read on, because if you dare to violate this place, inadvertently or otherwise, you could be responsible for unbalancing not just your partners spiritual equilibrium, but the matrix of the whole, unseen, universe.

Where can this holy place, this seat where communion occurs between the sons of men and God, be found?

Walk into your bedroom. Step around to the side the man sleeps on. If you will fix your gaze upon the space measuring about one and a half feet square which occurs to the side directly in line with his pillow, that, my friend, is it. You have before you Holy Ground.

The little place a man has beside his bed is consecrated. It is a kind of altar for sacrificing things on. When he buys something new from a shop, something that cost a lot or that he wanted for a really long time, it will go straight to the sacred spot and stay there for a while, like a kind of offering to the gods. It's as if he places it there just to see if God will take it away, and anything that God doesn't remove in a week can finally come off the altar, be used, eaten, written on, screwed up and/or thrown in a drawer or in the dirty clothes basket. If someone special gives him a card for his birthday or other occasion, that too will go in the spot for a while. It's a kind of testimony, evidence of their ability to invoke sincere feeling in others. See, God? I simply can't be an asshole all of the time - see what somebody gave me?

The blessed bit beside the bed is also the place to exhibit the works of ones hands - a kind of show-and-tell to God. When the man makes something at work that is particularly clever, he will bring it home and hurry it into the special spot. He knows that, like the tooth fairy checking for teeth, God checks the spot every night for special things needing his attention or approval. This is why you may be making the bed one day and find a piece of a machine, a manual with something underlined, or a particularly complicated piece of timber joinery neatly arranged on the floor next to the pillow. It will be discreetly taken away in about a week, once it's been blessed to be replaced with another item ready for inspection.

The bedside altar is also where things go which are proving a bit tricky for your man. A troublesome carburetor, tangled piece of rope or book that's a little bit beyond him will come to rest within the blessed cordon, until he receives a certain prompting that the grace needed for the job has been bestowed Zen-like while he was doing something else important, like sleeping. Don't solve the problem for him, or give your advice. Hard things put in the special space prove he is working on trusting God. It's a good thing.

He will make little offerings on his altar from time to time, in particular leaving half drunk cups of water like one might leave whiskey for Santa. You will have to remove these around the time dust starts to settle on the surface of the liquid because when this happens, both the water and the receptacle containing it have become invisible to him. While you can clearly see the cup and the water still sitting there, next to last weeks cup, he sincerely believes that after three days God drank his offering and also supernaturally took the cup. This is, and will always remain, a deep mystery - of course, I am speaking of the fact your man can't see the cup.

There are other objects that will from time to time come to be in the place beside his bed - artifacts from building sites and junkyards, bits of the natural world and other relics of humanity. This is his private study of sociology and philosophy. He has built a little anthropological study table there, and if you watch, you will see his whole life pass across it. You'll be tempted to remove the things, but do not give in to this. I would strongly suggest you observe carefully what he puts there, because everything that really matters to him will pass over this holiest of places at some time. Pieces of you, pieces of his family of origin, pieces of his children and his friends. He'll bring the fruit of his hands, things he finds interesting and the proof of his cleverness, and if you love this person, you'll take notice, and you'll respect and acknowledge the unseen velvet rope he's placed these things within as a necessary entity for him, and for the health of your relationship.

There are not many places in a man's life where he can be honest about who he really is and what he really cares about. Violating a man's bedside holy spot has worse implications than just making him annoyed, or forcing him to pocket things that will end up breaking your washing machine. If you impede his right to have public private space, mark my words, he will revert to *private* private space. And that will be much more upsetting than having a pile of nuts and bolts on the floor, I assure you.

My advice? Leave it alone. Thanks to Eve, I think we're in enough trouble as it is. I'd rather have an untidy little spot of Holy Ground in my house, even if it isn't mine, than a whole house clean and under control but without the kind of sublime chaos that makes bushes burst into flames and donkeys talk. How about you?

29

Why Christians Are Not The Boss Of Marriage

I've been doing some thinking about marriage lately, in light of the recent decision by New York State in the U.S. to legalise homosexual marriage, as reported by the New York Times.

I myself am married. I committed this act when I was all of nineteen years old. The person I married was just eighteen, and we had managed to make a little baby together the year before. Of all the things we did in those early years, marrying was certainly *technically* the easiest. It was one terrific day. But getting ourselves a Christian marriage had definitely been much harder, despite the fact we both wanted it, were old enough, heterosexual and Christian.

We knew we wanted to get married pretty much right after we found out I was pregnant with the little baby. It never occurred to us we should have an abortion, or adopt. We wanted to be together, and we wanted to put things right. We felt that our relationship had broken lots of rules, and violated people's expectations of us at that time. Whose rules? Whose expectations? Well, our families of origin, the church, and our peers at the youth group we belonged to. We wanted to let them all know we were prepared to do the right thing after being pretty much finished with doing the wrong thing. We figured we could be together, and have people think well of us again, by getting married all Christian-like.

But it proved not to be quite that simple. Just in case we'd made the grave mistake of thinking doing the right thing was as easy as doing the wrong thing, the leaders of our church youth group asked us to stand up in front of all our peers at the Friday night youth service and apologize to everyone for what we'd done. Right after vomiting from the sheer horror of it, we agreed to do it. We said sorry for letting everyone down, and explained to everyone how we fully intended to marry and make a family together. We thought the speech was going quite well when the assistant youth pastor stood up and remarked "Well, we'll just see how it goes, won't we?" I.e.: It's all right to say these things, but time will tell. Wow, we *so* want *you* to be our associate senior pastor in five years time. Not.

Getting everyone's approval was clearly going to be more difficult than we'd thought. Ever hopeful for the blessing of the church on our relationship, right after our lovely little baby was born we brought him to our church to ask our senior pastor if we could have a public dedication for him on a Sunday morning in church, just like everyone else. We were told to come back after we were married. Not long after that, our first piece of pre-marriage counseling included this little gem. "So, seeing as you two had sex before marriage, one of your big concerns will obviously be what other contraventions of God's laws you are capable of breaking. Are you at all concerned that the other may have affairs because both your ability to do the right thing is demonstrated to be so poor?" We didn't get any more counseling after that.

All of this hassle, just so *we* wouldn't be living *in sin*. So, just what do you call it when people take money for putting a young couple through that?

For years I had this morbid fear that perhaps the pastor who married my husband and I had forgotten to submit the paperwork to the authorities and we'd get a letter one day to say we weren't really married at all. I would lie in bed and worry about it, then one day I realized that if this were true, God already knew. Maybe *that's* why, I reasoned, everything is always going wrong for us? Maybe we never have any money and fight all the time because we are *still* sinful in the eyes of God?

Shame is a hard stain to shift.

*****

I believe in marriage, but I don't insist that others do. However, when people have said to me in the past that marriage is "just a piece of paper," I have been known to reply "so is a drivers license." I know we Christians have tried to tell people there are consequences for not getting the piece of paper and acting as if you are married, and we have given it a dirty name to make people feel bad for doing it. It's called "living in sin". But you don't stop living in sin once you get married, I can assure you. The piece of paper will not guarantee the level of maturity and wisdom required for a peaceful, non-combative partnership, but the way the church carries on you'd think a marriage license was some kind of diploma for emotional intelligence. It certainly ain't that.

I am actually still deciding if marriage is the exclusively "Christian" institution we have made it out to be. I've been doing some research trying to find out exactly when marriage as such began to be mentioned in the Bible. Old Testament marriages would certainly have been Judaic ceremonies: at least from the time Judaism began to be practiced. However, I find no evidence that Adam and Eve were Jewish, nor their direct descendants, so no such ceremony could have occurred in their instance, yet Adam is referred to as Eve's husband, and Eve as Adams wife as early as Genesis 3. Also, I cannot find a text for a marriage ceremony as such in the Bible. Marriage, wives and husbands just seem to start to be mentioned at some point, right back early in Genesis, way before the Mosaic Law, or Jewishness are.

Despite this Biblical ambiguity, Christians talk about marriage as if we invented it in the first place and only ever meant to loan it to the world, with the condition we always reserve the right to decide who gets to do it. However, practically every religion, people and culture in the world has its own marriage rites. Regardless, Christianity continue to claim their self-professed right to dictate the conditions of everyone's marriage in the whole world, even though marriage existed way before Christianity, before Judaism, even before people were separated by language, into tribes, cultural groups or nations and even before government. According to *the Bible*. I'm not making this up.

Whilst I can't understand Christian's meanness on marriage, I can understand why people who aren't allowed to get married would like to. There are various social and financial advantages for married couples, and I think everyone ought to be allowed to access these advantages if they are citizens of the society providing them. I do not believe that variances you were born with are sufficient qualification to exclude a person from marriage. The debate about inherent variances versus conscious choices will have to wait for another time, but suffice to say that even if being homosexual is a "lifestyle choice", it still doesn't mean human rights must relinquished in exchange for it, any more than choosing to become a Christian should, which, it could also be argued, is perhaps just as much a "life-style choice".

I've observed that Christians have a droll tendency to hoard up all the fun and special things in life like marriage and Christmas and being a family and call them Christian even though they're really not. The fact is you don't have to be a Christian to love someone, to be able to make a vow and keep it, to sign a contract or to even have a child. Marriage and family are not Christian institutions; they are human ones. It ought to be okay for all human beings to be able to get married if they want to, anyway they want to, for whatever reason they choose. Christians just don't get to make up the rules for all the human beings, any more than Buddhists or Muslims do. Boy, do we kick up a stink when they try it.

I believe that Christians, in their moral exuberance, must not require that the basic human rights and freedoms of non-Christians be diminished in any way unless they are prepared to give up their own rights and freedoms equally. Lord knows, we're not. A few months ago, a church in the town we were living protested publicly about a festival organised by the homosexual community that the council was considering approving. At the same time as they were protesting, this particular church enjoyed the blessing of the very same council for their own public Christmas celebration in December. However, the church did not recognise that in effect their protest against the homosexual event was absurd. They wanted the basic right of gay people to gather and celebrate and run a legal, family-oriented event in their town to be denied, whilst their own right to do the same be upheld. Ironically, later in the year and unrelated to the protest, the local business that had sponsored the church event withdrew their support, and Carols by Candlelight had to be cancelled. However, the gay event went ahead, and was a great success.

You know, in another time and place, not very long ago, people with dark skin were not allowed to marry one another, or anyone else. Instead, they were obliged to continue to live and work in an elite, aloof, and very Christian society that made them into pariahs and slaves. However, these people, the ones whom they said were not even qualified to be called human, married each other in secret and lived as married people just the same. The stupid, white, religious people who said they couldn't just had to suck it up and get the hell over it.

I believe history may be about to repeat itself.

My marriage is one of the things that has made me the happiest – and also the most miserable – in my life, but if I have taken it for granted in the past, I do so no longer. This isn't just because of the trials we have been through to stay together, but also because I cannot imagine what it might have been like if we had been forbidden to marry in the first place. For me now to think that some people in my community are denied the right to marry for what I consider fairly redundant reasons almost makes me want to divorce on principle. It's not that I hold contempt for marriage, on the contrary, but I do hold contempt for the conditions others place upon it in the name of the Christ I follow, a Christ who has shown to me nothing but love, compassion, acceptance, leadership, support, forgiveness and mercy.

Marriage is an institution I have come to respect and revere, and which has afforded me social privileges which prior to now, I hadn't even considered would have been withheld if the person I loved and had children with were a woman. My conscience and my Christianity prevents me from continuing to passively accept these privileges I enjoy without ensuring they are also available to others if I can see no reason, political, moral or otherwise, why they ought to be withheld. Christians may continue to deny the rights of others in the community to marry, claiming marriage is a Christian institution, but Biblically, marriage was a human institution way before it was ever a Christian one. I believe Christians need to be careful they do not stray back into the stupid, white, religious practices that have alienated many people from the church in the past. I conclude with a favorite quote of mine from Anne Lamott: you can be sure your God is a god of your own invention when it turns out he hates all the same people you do.

30

Why I Don't Blame You For Thinking The Bible Is Stupid

People sometimes do funny things with their Bibles. Apart from using them occasionally to cover stains on the back seat of the car, or place between Rob Bell's latest book and the coffee table to stop a portal to hell from being scorched into it's surface (if hell really exists, that is), the Bible is also often widely used to support a whole range of views and opinions ranging from the sacred to the obscene. The thing with the Bible is that, unlike books written by authors who are still alive, we can't ask the people who wrote it what they really meant when they said certain stuff. However, I happen to think their absence is insufficient license, poetic or otherwise, for the amount of liberties Christians in particular are wont to take with what they often refer to, ironically, as the unchanging Word of God.

I actually think many Christians like to pretend reading the Bible is much harder than it really is, but it's really not *that* hard. Many regular people not claiming to be Christian, or even especially religious, don't seem to have as much trouble working out what the Bible is about as most Christians think they might, or would perhaps prefer they did. I know people who just picked up a Bible one day and started reading, and didn't have any real issues understanding it as either a work of literature, as a spiritual guide, or as a historical document. And don't we Christians just hate that. We'd like the Bible to be *special*, something only we truly understand and appreciate. I think a lot of the readings we make of scripture are really just our own attempt to make ourselves feel superior and other people feel excluded, which is kind of the opposite of what the Bible is about in the first place, when you think about it.

Now, I admit that some parts of the Bible are more difficult to read than others. Chapters like Revelation are certainly fodder for interesting interpretation, as can those bits of the Bible be which might act as a metaphor for the relationship between Christ and the church (the sexy bits) like Song of Solomon. Sure, these particular chapters can, and perhaps should, be exegeted several ways. But Christians are prone to smirk that people reject the Bible simply because they haven't got the special spiritual beer-goggles for it, you know, the ones you get when you "become a Christian". However, I've found a lot of people reject the Bible wholesale not because of what they think it says about them personally, but actually because of what we Christians tell them what we personally think it says about them. Like God can't stand them, for example.

In my experience, many not-Christians who have taken the time to read the Bible go on to reject it not because they don't understand it, as Christians like to think, but because they find it 1) largely irrelevant (they don't see is as having much practical use in their lives) 2) strangely incomplete (they find out that lots of books were considered for inclusion, but didn't make the cut, and they don't understand how Christians can accept this without question) and 3) has been over-interpreted to the point of distortion largely by people who have concluded that God only loves the people who think, act and read the Bible the same way they do. And I think they'd be pretty much right on all three counts.

I think we Christians have sometimes been guilty of making the Bible into a kind of exclusive handbook for our special club complete with secret codes, rules and complex initiation ceremonies. When we can't find in the handbook exactly what we're looking for, we just find a way to make it say what we need it to say, usually to exclude someone we don't like or are afraid of. Not one for tattoos? Found a bit that supports that in Leviticus. Prone to misogynist swinery? Found some support for you also. Hate homosexuals? Oh, big fat check on that. Believe, perchance, that God wants to give you everything your little heart desires, regardless of how trivial, materialistic, selfish or stupid it is? *Well, duh.* Of course the Bible says that.

Christians deny they ever take liberties with scripture, but we do, regardless of the fact we've also said that scripture is God-breathed, inerrant and eternal. If we agree with a particular distortion, we call it a *revelation,* and the prophet said to be *anointed.* If we don't agree, it's an *apostasy* and the utterer is a *heretic.* While Bible scholars might argue that we can never really know the intended meaning of much of scripture, there are surely instances when we can be pretty certain we are not using it the way the author intended. I think we can be sure we have used a scripture out of context when the twenty or so words that appear before it, and the twenty or so words that come after it, mean exactly the opposite of the twenty or so words we've plucked out of the middle to support our particular opinion on something. A lot of very well qualified pastors I know in real life use passages from scripture in fairly erroneous fashion. So ambivalent and creative are their interpretations one wonders why they bothered to use the Bible to support their statements, when your basic, everyday, high-quality supermarket catalogue might have served the same purpose, with much less confusion.

Ben and I once visited a church we were thinking of attending (we'd just moved to town) and, isn't it always the way, that morning the pastor was delivering the exciting new plan for the church building project. He was encouraging the church to not feel that their very ambitious and expensive building program was out of their reach technically or financially, and exhorting them to believe that God Himself appreciated they could achieve their goal despite all the obstacles. His scripture reference? Genesis 11:6. "Nothing they plan to do will be impossible for them!" His passage of choice comes from the story of the tower of Babel. In the preceding scripture, God has come down to check out a huge idolatrous monolith the people are building, and in the following one, God supernaturally confuses their language so they can't understand each other, and the building project is abandoned. The people are then scattered across the face of the earth. If the church had been a little smaller than the five hundred or so people present that morning, they might have heard me laughing, but they might have just confused it for the hilarious, giving the pastor was enthusiastically encouraging at the time. Whilst I certainly advocate for scripture reading that isn't brain surgery, surely we can do better than this proverbial psycho-style stab in the dark.

Apart from the outright decontextualisation of scripture, there are those faithful old chestnuts we've pulled out of the Bible for everyday, albeit incongruous, use. There's that all-time Pentecostal classic, "I can do all things through Christ who strengthens me", a particular favorite of my husband's. It's his favorite because he always gets a belly laugh at the various ways people use it usually to support things Christians want very much to do but find themselves unable to. Like parking anywhere they want without getting a ticket, or beating someone they hate at a game. "I can do all things through Christ" has come to mean "I'll be able to do whatever its takes to get myself out of this present situation, which I find intolerable, with Jesus' help. Because naturally He wants for me the same thing I want for myself – wealth, comfort and no one who disagrees with my views." However, a closer reading of this particular part of Philippians reveals that Paul is talking about being able to *make himself content* in the midst, and able to tolerate all manner, of human tribulation, through his faith in Christ. Rather than saying, "This is crap, I'm blasting my way outta here with my special, Jesussy super-powers", Paul is actually saying "I have learned to be content whatever the circumstances, and boy, is Jesus Christ a big help with that." So as it turns out it's his own propensity for discontentment, and not the problems irritating him that are actually the big problem he needs Jesus' help with. Funny, that.

The Bible isn't stupid. If you thought it was, can I just say it's not God's fault, and that Christians in my opinion have a case to answer. I think it's time the faithful faced the fact that sometimes we don't know exactly what the Bible means, as clearly demonstrated by our changing it around an awful lot to make it say pretty much whatever we'd like it to. Christians must also admit that the Bible was far more likely given us to help us understand who and what God is, and not merely to indicate where He stands in relation to our own wants, our own plans, our own problems and our own ambitions. In other words, the Bible is *not always about us*, people. Also, the Bible is not actually as complex as we've sometimes been led to believe, and I believe it's neither as shallow as others appear to want us to think. If God gave the Bible to the world, as we claim He did, it's my belief that He was forward thinking enough to make it equitably accessible to everyone with enough wherewithal to read it. Plainly and simply.

We do not always understand the Bible, but we must resist dumbing it down and twisting it around to suit our white, middle-class, Western, heterosexual, democratic agenda, as if God were any of these things. We can only ever see scripture as we do everything else sacred or otherwise in this world – in a mirror darkly – and we will probably all face-palm in eternity when God is able to explain what He really meant in Revelation after all. Myself, I find my Bible to be mystical enough to convince me people must have needed God's help to write it, and shallow enough that I am reassured He didn't lower himself to say many of the stupid things Christians claim He did.

31

It's Not Spiritual

If it lifts me up, and puts you down, it's not spiritual.

If it separates and divides us from each other, it's not spiritual.

If it makes me better than you, or makes you better than me, it's not spiritual.

If it disconnects me from creation, or separates me from creativity, it's not spiritual.

If it can only be defined by how much of it can be possessed or purchased, it's not spiritual.

If I can never be as good at it as you are, it's not spiritual.

If who and what I am right now isn't a step on the way to it, it's not spiritual.

If I have to go to it, and it can never come to me, it's not spiritual.

If the only way to it is through the intellect, through my comprehension, through cleverness and deftness and expertise, it's not spiritual.

If it can be fully known, it's not spiritual.

If I am intrinsically diminished as a human being, or made superior to other human beings by it, it's not spiritual.

If you can keep me from it, and if you can rob me of it, it's not spiritual.

If the only way I can attain it is through you, it's not spiritual.

If you can show me where it begins and where it ends, it's not spiritual.

If your vocabulary is sufficient to describe it, it's not spiritual.

If it can comfortably exist side by side with fear, prejudice, judgment and hatred, it's not spiritual.

If I talk about it and you can't understand what I'm on about, it's not spiritual.

If it disappears the second I leave the place I claim to have found it, it's not spiritual.

If language can define it, bigotry malign it, pride undermine it and religion assign it, it's definitely, absolutely, categorically not spiritual.

32

And Then Jesus Said Thank You For My Socks

At the moment in my job, I'm working at a 24-hour mental health facility with some folks who have what's known as a dual diagnosis. This means they have an initial mental illness diagnosis, usually schizophrenia, along with something else as well, like ADHD, autism, or an intellectual disability. Talk about your busy day, and that's just for the clients.

This new role is pretty intense – much more intense than my last job. Schizophrenia is an asshole, and people who have to live with it seem to me a lot like a displaced tribe of refugees from another dimension. It's like they arrived alone and without luggage from somewhere nobody ever heard of - a place where nobody lives indoors, where just about everybody needs nicotine like they need oxygen and it's quite normal to carry demons with you everywhere nestled in the folds of your ears.

When supporting someone with schizophrenia, you find yourself doing a lot of housework, because disorganization is one side effect of the disorder. You might also spend vast amounts of time avoiding inhaling the pall of cigarette smoke that often surrounds your client. You may also spend a lot of time and energy competing with someone you can neither hear nor see, and absolutely cannot acknowledge, for the attention of their host. It's not so much annoying as it is completely heartbreaking, and enraging. I want to smash schizophrenia in the head, but from what I have observed, it's already got what I want to give it. For all the difficulty I have dealing with the voices my clients tell me they hear, I can't imagine what it must be like to live with the things those voices say to them. It's never "have a great day, pal", or "you're awesome, you know that?" From what I'm told, the voices are commonly acutely malicious and subversive. "That person wants to kill you, but you can hurt them first." "You're so stupid, when are you ever going to learn what I tell you is the truth?" "Everyone is listening, nowhere is safe." One client needs me stay close when she goes grocery shopping, because her voices tell her to bite the other shoppers. She is a gentle and shy lady, and doesn't want to bite the other shoppers, and so being told she ought to do that by someone inside her head is obviously very troubling for her. Another believes that because of the strict gun laws that exist in Australia, the people who are trying to locate and kill him are waiting with chain saws behind every corner. They want to kidnap him and make him participate in a snuff porn movie. Imagine living with those thoughts inside your head, with varying amounts of insight into whether what you're thinking is real, or not, as you go about your day.

There's stressful, and there's stressful.

195

I haven't much idea how I've ended up doing this job - I have no real qualifications or experience but applied anyway - all I can say is that it just "feels right." I've managed to bluff my way into both the organizations I've worked for this year with vicarious talk of my ability to "think on my feet" and how I'm "great with people". I've not told them about the voices in my own head. I have, however, shared in my job interviews how I think maybe my personal experience with mental illness and anxiety, and being married to someone who has been both an addict and suffered from depression, might have put me in some good stead. There have been three specific times lately when God has clearly shown me I am here to learn something I don't know.

One. I'm visiting a particular client for the first time. She is a young woman, about thirty, a striking and formidable figure physically, and spiritually. When I'm with this client, I never ever feel in control - it's as though she is tolerating me, allowing me the barest level of engagement, patronizing me because I can serve her wants and needs. And I'm totally okay with that. Truth be known, I'm in awe of her. This first time I get to be in her apartment, I am looking around the place cautiously, because with a person who has schizophrenia, you never know if what you see is what they see. The kitchen table is covered with various objects and plant cuttings in assorted containers, and several hand drawn pictures of animals and tribal figures are stuck to the wall behind it. A small dish holding four, huge ripe plums. "I guess this is your dining table, then." Wrong. "That", says the client "is my shrine. And that", she indicates to where I am standing in front of her shrine "is where I pray. Every day I kneel right there and I pray and give thanks to God. I thank Him for everything in this world, and for who I am, and tell him how great I think He is." A shiver goes down my spine. And I bet God listens, too. I suddenly have tan urge to take off my shoes. Holy ground.

Two. I'm chatting with a new client and we realize, to our amusement and surprise, we share a birthdate. Same day, month, year. I ask her where she grew up, what she used to do for fun, what music she likes. We sunbaked on the same patch of beach, bought our Alpines 25's from the same corner shop, roller-skated at the same rink. Both of us married when we were nineteen. We both have four kids, all around the same ages. Spooky, and it's not lost on us. As we drive along listening to Cyndi Lauper on the radio up way too loud with the windows down, our sunglasses on and the breeze in our hair, I wonder if we're thinking the same thing. Which of us ended up with God's grace?

Three. Tonight, I am helping an elderly male client get ready for bed. He's toothless, incontinent and absolutely gorgeous. I reckon he was once a street fighter - his nose is boneless and flat like a squashed mandarin, and he has part of an ear missing. I've shepherded him out of his shower and wrestled him into jammies, beanie and dressing gown, and I'm kneeling on the floor pulling his socks onto his waxy, knobbly feet. As he gently rests his foot in my palm, I am reminded of Jesus washing his disciples feet, and of the time when He said 'I tell you, whatever you did for one of the least of these brothers and sisters of mine, you did for me.' And just as that moment, the voices in my own head kick in.

"Hey - it's me, Jesus. Just wanted to say, thank you for my socks."

33

Speaking In Tongues, Internet Shopping,

And My Three Nights On The Mental Health Ward

The mental health organisation I am working for at the moment has a 24-hour facility with clients living on site. These particular clients require around the clock care and supervision because of their dual diagnosis. These darling folks (and I mean that most sincerely) can't be left alone for a moment, otherwise they may wander off and do various anti-social things out in the neighbourhood, the details of which I won't elaborate on. Suffice to say, staff have a lockable office on the block of housing units that a staff member must man overnight. Our job is to ensure to make sure nobody supposed to be staying leaves, and more importantly, make sure nobody comes on site that doesn't belong. I'm told this has happened in the past. This is a fairly high crime neighbourhood with vandalism and robberies commonplace. There was a stabbing murder just down the street a few weeks ago. This thought comforts the staff no end at two in the morning when we're locked in the teensy little office watching late-night movies with one eye on the grainy security monitor and one hand clutching a fistful of keys like a set of knuckledusters.

On the whole, this role is turning out to be a little more demanding than I bargained for. I applied for a part-time position. I thought that meant I'd be working part of every week. My employer, however, seems to believe it means part of every day. I had no idea I'd even be doing night shifts when I applied, but thought it might be an interesting experience. On receiving my roster, I was surprised to discover I have about six overnight shifts every three weeks, and three of those shifts are consecutive - a Friday, Saturday and a Sunday night all one after the other.

My first triple night shift was last weekend. 11pm to 7am, all of it to be done sitting up or walking around, absolutely wide-awake. There are rounds to be walked, and paperwork to be signed to say rounds have been walked. I thought I'd be a little scared staying awake there by myself all night, but then I realized that being asleep, or even half asleep there by myself all night would be much, much worse. I packed myself a lunch bag with some appetising snacks, because if there's anything I know will help keep me awake it's the thought that several varieties of tasty food are available and nearby. I also packed my computer, hoping to catch up on a little writing. Over the next three nights I was to experience a weird kind of menopausal, mental-ward, twilight-zone.

My first night on site I decided to watch a few movies I'd brought with me. My kids had suggested I rent such horror slash drama epics as Gothika (set in a mental hospital, I'm told), Jason Returns (featuring a certain psychotic homicidal maniac) and perhaps even One Flew Over The Cuckoos Nest (where a sane but pathologically irritating guy fakes mental illness and ends up with a lobotomy). I've since decided on a black ban against any movie with Jack Nicholson in it, because when the gentleman from unit four comes shuffling up to the glass door in the wee hours to ask for a smoke and protest against his treatment it makes me feel just like Nurse Ratchet.

At first, I thought I seemed to be coping quite well with being awake all night, three nights in a row. The Friday night shift came and went. I slept after arriving home about 7:15am Saturday morning, then got up about 11am and did some stuff until having an early dinner at 6pm and heading back to bed. I got up at 10:30pm and got ready for work at 11pm. Then I did it again for Saturday night and Sunday night.

Monday morning arrived. Everyone was getting ready for work and school when I got home just after seven in the morning. I felt like I had passed through weary, beyond tired, kicked exhausted's ass and now I was all fired up and ready to roll. I bounced around my family like a puppy. "Where ya goin'? Where ya goin'? Gosh ya lookin' awesome! Wow, what a beautiful day, don't ya think!? Where ya headed? Goin' out? Can I come? Can I come?" The last one to leave kicked me off their leg after dragging me up the hall, and locked the door from the outside shouting back at me, "Go to bed!" My eye-motes were vibrating. "Look at the sunshine! Look at the big blue-ness thingy! I'm so thirsty. I feel so skinny! I don't need to sleep, I need eggs. I have a car! I can go out and drive and get eggs! That's not me that smells, no way. I'm going for eggs!"

At a nearby café, I found eggs, poached ones, two of them, on top of a slice of sourdough on a very white plate beside a rustic hand-thrown terracotta receptacle which held about a cup of home-made baked beans. There was garnish. And relish made from an exotic berry. My coffee hummed in my teeth while I batted my eyelids at the staff flirtatiously. I watched a video clip on my phone without the sound with my jaw hanging open, and read my local paper with the perplexity of a jet-lagged tourist - what day is it here? I then gave the lady at the cash register all my petrol money for my breakfast, and went looking for an art supplies shop.

I spent enough to get five holes punched in a brand new customer loyalty card.

Now, I know better. On the next post-triple-shift Monday morning, I must have an arrangement in place with someone I trust to take my credit card and my car keys away, put snacks in my bed, to which they must forcibly direct me, after they have me change out of my underwear, just in case I hallucinated I was camping on Saturday night and have been turning them inside out ever since. I have also closed all my internet shopping accounts, just in case. I think probably 95% of purchases made on Ebay are by shift workers after their thirty-six hour rotation.

I have a theory now that in Acts, when the disciples spoke in tongues in the upper room, it wasn't so much the holy spirit as the fact they'd pulled a couple of chronic all-niters, shut in a room surrounded by mental health patients and potentially axe-murdering cat-burglars. Think about it. No sleep, three nights in a row. Small, enclosed space. Not long since having been with someone claiming to be Jesus Christ. Sounds very much like my three-night weekend on the mental health ward.

34

Seven Reasons Why I Am A Bad Christian Wife

1) I don't care much for being cute.

I'm a Christian wife, mother and a writer, but believe me, I don't look like Lisa Bevere. I have several tattoos, long, blonde dreadlocks and I wear size 14. I found out that American clothes size numbers are smaller than Australian ones, so I'm trying to get my husband to move us to Portland, Oregon (in the US) so I can email everyone back home in Australia and tell them I have instantly become a size 10. Having dreadlocks means I save a heap on shampoo, styling product and haircuts, and I plan to spend what I save on those for the move to Portland. I hear they're real big on things like tattoos and dreadlocks there.

2) I never make my husbands lunches.

We married on a sunny February morning, on a Saturday. I made my husbands first lunch to take to work on the Monday following our return from our honeymoon. On Friday of the same week, my husband came home from work and said he didn't like what I was giving him for lunch. That was in 1989, and is, my friend, how you get back fifteen minutes of your day and avoid a hell of a lot of shouting.

3) I hate to cook.

For some reason, Christian women are supposed to like cooking, and are supposed to cook a variety of nutritious tasty food for their families and provide same for sick members of the church community and the occasional pot luck dinner. I've given it a red-hot try over the years, believe me, but I'm still just not into it. All that time and energy, for something that will be devoured in under a minute. And that's if they *like* it. Heaven forbid you should throw in something new every once in a while. Totally discouraged in the end by my family's resistance to all experimentation mainly designed to try and keep up my own motivation, I resorted to cooking the same five things in rotation. After eating this menu for years, our older kids are now physically allergic to tuna casserole. I believe my spaghetti Bolognese is probably responsible for my adult sons suspected coeliac disease.

On the upside, my husband and kids have decided that there are other ways to get interesting and tasty food. Make it themselves, or order it in. My evil plan is working.

4) I don't go to Christian Women's Conferences.

Large groups of just women - and Christian women particularly - make me very, very nervous. I prefer to stay home with my man and practice on my own marriage than I do sitting in a big room and listening to the pastors wife talk about hers.

5) I'm not bothered by my husband's sexual needs.

Most of the books I've read for Christian women on the subject of sex make the assumption that there will be problems in the marriage because he is going to want so much of it. Maybe there is something wrong, because my husbands needs have never been a problem for me. Oh yes, I'm a *bad* Christian wife.

6) I don't like to entertain.

I think this is mostly because I am afraid of being judged, because I am not a very good housekeeper. You're not even at my house, and you're judging me now because of what I just told you, I know it. You really want to be in the house, eating the cupcakes and sipping the tea of someone with so many neuroses? Of course not. I realise this, and so I have mercifully spared us both the embarrassment. Not entertaining is good for my marriage because my husband likes me better when my neurosis are not aggravated. That will work.

7) I swear. A lot.

Clearly this makes it difficult for me to be a Really Good Christian Wife. I could be a really good bowery sea captain, however. My tattoos, I believe, help significantly. My penchant for coarse language benefits our marriage because my husband need have no fear I will be stolen away by another man, at least not a tender-hearted one. I wouldn't stand for being stolen away anyway. I'm also a bit of a shin-kicker.

I'm not really that bad of a Christian wife, my husband says, but he also said that these seven things are probably only funny if you don't have to live them. That was right before I told him to shut up and eat his tuna casserole.

Ps: If you punch "good Christian wife" into Google images, funnily enough you get a whole lot of pictures of Christian Bale, who coincidentally looks remarkably like my husband Ben, and on whom I have a very famous crush. How serendipitous :)

35

Nothing Tastes As Good As Watching

A Skinny Girl Eat Her Heart Out

You know one of my pet hates? Women, usually TV presenters, who have never known what it's like to be overweight, publicly making their own grand commentary about things concerning larger women. It's like having your local Catholic priest give you marriage advice. Exactly what the heck would *you know about it*?

Maybe they feel they are qualified because they have, as they describe it, *struggled* with their weight in the past. But I doubt this would be *struggled* as in struggled to get a coffee if the barista is male and under twenty-five, struggled into what *looks* like a perfectly averaged size 14 pair of jeans or struggled to look the sales assistant in the eye when she has brought to the change room *everything we have in store in your size* and still, nothing fits. Maybe they think they can weigh (pardon the pun) into the argument on the basis of how many emotional and physical resources they have shoved maniacally at preventing even the tiniest amount of fatness, as if not having a space between your thighs when you stand with your knees together were a form of cancer. It just makes me laugh when someone who has obviously never really been classified as overweight tells everyone how we ought to treat overweight people. As someone who has been classified as overweight for much of my adult life, I can tell you that this doesn't really feel like support. It feels like *patronization*.

There have been times when I have *struggled* with being overweight, but I don't fight against myself like that any more. My body deserves much, much better. I've grown to consider my body to be pretty much my hero. When I think about it, it's done some amazing things, including giving birth to four children and surviving cancer. I am actually tired of beating it up, hating it and wishing it looked like someone else's.

I'm 5'4", size 14-16 (Australian size) and about 76kgs. Not thin. I'm not hugely obese either, but I think that's probably as much about genes and luck as good management. I am too busy to get really fat, but I like my food too much to be really thin. I am simply not prepared to take my attention off other things that interest me and refocus on getting into size 10 jeans. It's tempting for me to defend the things that take my attention away from making myself thinner in some kind of sanctimonious light, but I actually shouldn't need to paint myself as Mother Theresa. So I'm fat. I haven't done anything *wrong*.

Yep, that's right. Being bigger than an XS is not actually a moral defect. It does mean I can't get a job as a magazine model, and it may even mean that men in the street will pass me over as a prospective sexual partner, but I think I'm pretty okay with that. I have often wondered why, in this age of supposed women's liberation, many women are still not liberated from the idea that a woman's existence on the earth is validated only if someone visually assesses us in five seconds as a viable sexual object when they walk past us in the street. And I also do not understand why a viable sexual partner is defined as someone who has visible collarbones, invisible cellulite (let's face it, every woman has it) and can buy their jeans from the single digit end of the rack. For all intents and purposes, a woman who owns wobbly upper arms can still participate in fabulous, mutually gratifying sex. Take my word for it, she absolutely can. And should.

A lot of the neurosis I've had about my weight lately has been because I've felt I had a lack of neurosis about my weight, and I wondered if that was actually normal. *Just look at yourself, how can you not be dieting - what the hell is wrong with you?* As I grow older, I've fostered a philosophy of living my life from the inside out - that is, I believe my body exists to carry my *self* around in, and not the other way around. It's my *self that* loves my children and my husband, and tries to be a better human being. It's my *self* that works hard to remember I must eat fruit more often than I eat banana bread, because banana bread is not really fruit, and my body doesn't work properly if I don't eat enough fruit. It's my *self* that goes off to work each day as a mental health support worker, and tries hard to connect with the selves inside the other bodies of the people I work with that don't work the way the owners wish they would. It's my *self* that communes with my God, and prays and worships and thanks Him for the life I have, for my second chance to be here. Its my *self* that cares for my body, physically and spiritually, and appreciates that I will only be able to do what I want to do if my body is healthy enough to take me where I want to go. It's my *self*, having been fed and nourished just as well as my physical body, that appreciates looking good in a bikini isn't ever going to be worth more than knowing how to be generous, grateful, forgiving, patient, kind and loving. Ever.

I look forward to a time when thinner women don't feel the need to advocate for we larger women - not because larger women are off our fat behinds and doing it for themselves, but because all women refuse to participate in a worldview that perpetuates issue with the relative weight of women in the first place. We have been divided into two groups - the relatively small and the relatively large. Relative to what? Each other? We cannot profess unity as a gender when it is we who maintain the mythical divide.

Women on the whole must change they way they think about what it means to be a woman. Sex and fat have become inextricably linked in women's minds. *If we can get sex, we are viable. If we are fat, we don't get sex.* This is technically untrue, and just lain stupid, but is the accepted mythology of our culture. Advertisers know it, and they make a shit load lot of money off of keeping it that way. They know that if women ever come to accept themselves the way they are, the entire economy of the Western world would collapse.

In any case, I find it slightly offensive that other women, particularly the thin ones with jobs on TV, assume they need to defend my size on my behalf. Please don't. I can actually do it. Despite my apparent size, I was physically able to get out of bed this morning believe it or not. I don't spend my days languishing on the sofa eating bon-bons. I can fight my own battles. We are not a silent minority you need to advocate for. Just because you can't see any fat people in your immediate vicinity please don't assume we are all lying in hot baths trying to open up a vein.

I think many thin women have made some broad and very negative assumptions about what it feels like to be fat, and based their well-meaning comments on them. They think *"being fat must be simply awful - after all, I can't think of anything worse - therefore I, being the thin person every fat person surely wishes they were, must step in and defend the rights of fat women."* Do us a favour - get over it. Get over my being fat. And further, get over your being thin. There's actually a lot to be said for an imposing physical presence. I have actually wondered if our society's obsession with female thin-ness is not merely some perverted way of making females appear collectively less threatening. Some women certainly act like being thin is the same thing as having a university degree or bringing about world peace. Well, you certainly may take up less space, but there is more than one way to be *lightweight*.

So, thin lady? Please don't stick up for me. Don't presume I have low self-esteem simply because I have a big, wide arse. Don't assume that I particularly want to see *curvy* models on catwalks so I can feel *normal*. I am not interested in magazines, models, catwalks or finding something that tastes as good as having a boney backside feels. Honey, you can eat your heart out. A lot of thin women are more sensitive about my weight than I am.

Thin lady on TV? Don't make your issues with your own weight into a political cause you need to defend on my behalf. I don't need you to stick up for me, honey. I'm not a silent, disempowered minority, and I don't need your advocacy. I don't look at you and feel bad about myself. I look at you and feel happy that I won't have to fight you for frozen desserts in the supermarket freezer section. You ought to feel good about this too, because although I could snap you like a twig, I'm too happy about being able to eat frozen desserts whenever I like to ever get *that* angry.

36

Because I'm Worth More Than That

This morning on the Australian Today Show, presenter Lisa Wilkinson made one of the best comments I've heard yet regarding women and body image.

"Any woman who doesn't celebrate celebrating another birthday needs to visit a cancer ward."

Amen, sister.

I spent a total of nine months in a cancer ward in 2003/2004 having treatment for stage 3B Non-Hodgkin's Lymphoma, and I've also spent a lot of time since then with hundreds of women who have had a cancer diagnosis. It changes you. In more ways than you could ever imagine.

Post cancer and treatment, my whole attitude to my own body changed dramatically. As far as I am concerned, my body is a wonderful thing, and I love it to pieces. It's had five children inside it, borne four of them live and wriggling out its front bottom, been sliced up and had things scooped out of it, and its almost checked-out a few times. Despite it all, it has bravely hung in there, regardless of how I largely treated it with scorn and disdain, refused to care for it properly and even cursed it under lights in a change room. Even when it got cancer, my body was tough enough to stand everything we threw at it, and thankfully, surprisingly, it didn't die. I think my body deserves a little better treatment than to be dieted and despised down into some scrap of nylon worth about four dollars, or hated because it's wrinkled, flabby and has a few scars. Most women treat their dogs better than their own bodies. My body is my hero.

You know, I would love a job on television. Not just because I think I look pretty terrific on TV (I have been on TV), but because I would love to have the opportunity to demonstrate to all those women who think they have to change themselves that it is possible to be content, successful, loved, happy and comfortable in a body, and with a face, that has seen a few miles and a few trials. Hire me, Television Producer Person, and I will tell and show your audience that it is possible to be active, relevant, intelligent, vital,

 loved and loving, beautiful and joyful in a middle aged woman's body complete with cellulite and uneven skin tone, undeterminable abs and boobs that resemble socks filled with sand. Your advertisers will hate me. I promise you - your viewers will love me.

Warning, Television Producer Person - I have dreadlocks. I'd wanted them for years, but was too afraid of being judged to give up my glossy, straight hair. What would people think? Screw 'em. I've never loved my hair more than I do now. I also have tattoos. Big ones. The first one I got was my whopping big "SURVIVOR" tattooed down my left forearm. I got it because what I have managed to survive in my life is exactly what I need to remember every day when I start judging myself because my house is dirty, or punishing myself because my abs aren't rock hard and my skin isn't flawless.

Oh, *I'm worth it,* as the cosmetic advertisement says - but I'm worth far more than wrinkle-obscuring make-up and image-changing hair colour. I am worth honouring, I am worth treasuring. I am worthy of respect and admiration - mine, and others. I'm worth much more than make-up and hair colour, worth more than criticism and judgment - yes, *mine, and others.*

When I look at my face in the mirror and see another wrinkle, or the places where my neck is beginning to sag, or a grey hair, I look down at the "survivor" tattoo on my arm - and at my scars where they took out the things that threatened to kill and maim me, and at my round tummy where my babies were, and at the big, floppy breasts that nursed them, and at the flabby arms that have hugged children and friends and held my husband close, and at the short, chubby legs that have carried me through trials I

217

never believed I would be able to endure - and I remember *I am tough, I am beautiful, I am sexy, I am amazing, I am a survivor.*

And I am worth more than that.

37

Sometimes The Hardest Thing About Being A Woman

Is The Blunt Object She's Swinging At Your Head

Sometimes, it's hard to be a woman. And sometimes, you just have to wonder why exactly that is. I don't make it hard. I have a vested interest in it being as easy as possible. It's everyone else that's stuffing it up. In fact, I think it's the crap I have to do around here simply because I have the breasts that makes being a woman far harder than necessary.

Apparently, washing and drying clothes takes a set of breasts, as does picking teenagers up from work. Dragging a cloth impregnated with cleaning fluid over a surface stained with dropped food requires a set of mammary glands too. And I know this is an old gripe, but removing a cardboard roll from beside a toilet, which once held a roll of paper that wipes every single other persons backside as well? You definitely have to have boobs for that. And did you know you absolutely need a great rack to be able to tell when food needs to be thrown out in the fridge? Neither did I. Apparently, if you don't have breasts, bagged lettuce so wilted it's become a foul-smelling green liquid is rendered invisible to your eyes. No need to throw out the bag! Just pop it back in there and shut the drawer.

And if you don't have tits, you can leave those mayonnaise boogers on the nozzle of the bottle, and those scabs on the sauce bottles too, and *absolutely nothing will happen*. One day, they just disappear all by themselves, probably to the same place where a mans snotty tissues go when he stuffs them under the seat of the couch. Poof! Those are some of life's great mysteries.

I bet those men who wish they were women and get themselves a set of boobs don't find themselves suddenly expected to wipe up random puddles of urine on the bathroom floor. I bet the kind of men who get boobs have worked out how not to make those puddles in the first place. Not necessarily because they are more feminine than other men, but because they are less *canine*. What kind of domesticated creature urinates on a floor? Why can a grown man throw a basketball the length of a court into a metal ring, but the same man can't aim a stream of fluid coming from his own body through a long tube into a hole the size of a basketball, mere inches away?

Only a bitch with boobs would make that kind of observation. Oh yes, it's hard to be a woman.

38

A Cancer Death Does Not A Hero Make

News reports today share the sad new that Steve Jobs, co-founder of Apple, has passed away after a long illness. Jobs, it's reported, had pancreatic cancer, a particularly insidious form of the disease.

The particular headline I read stated Jobs "lost his fight" against cancer.

The media uses this terminology a lot, but I find that people in real life – particularly those who have cancer or who work with those who have it – don't. The hairs stand up on the back on my neck whenever I read a headline like that. Not because someone died of cancer, although I do feel sad when this happens, but because of this word "*fight*" that is always used in association with it.

Fighting connotes a struggle is taking place, that resistance against an unwanted foe is in play. Of course, no one ever wants to have cancer. *But does everyone always not want to die?*

Why, when someone dies of cancer, do we say they "lost their fight"? Did they see themselves as a conquered victim? Did they pass away thinking they were vanquished or defeated just because they died? Are people who die *losers*?

Everyone dies. It's difficult to deal with finding out you will probably die in a manner not of your choosing, before you did everything you wanted to do. I know, because I was diagnosed with advanced cancer in 2003, and am now in remission. I am offended by the idea we perpetuate that when someone dies of cancer, cancer is somehow *the winner over them*. No, cancer is not. There are no winners and losers in cancer, unless the person with the cancer thinks this mindset helps them stay mentally strong. Surviving certainly doesn't mean you're a winner, any more than dying somehow means you're somehow a loser.

We cannot know Jobs' state of mind at the time of his death, but we do know he was financially comfortable and achieved a great deal in his lifetime. Perhaps he was ready to die, willing even. Perhaps he died with acceptance and grace. That would make him as great in his passing as he was in his lifetime. We know that as well as having a good life, it is possible to have a good death.

Yes, it's possible to have a good death.

A good death is one where a person has been able to come to accept what is happening to them. A good death is one where you are able to extend mercy to those who have wronged you in your lifetime. A good death is one where you are able to accept forgiveness for all the wrongs you have committed, particularly toward others. A good death is one where loose ends are tied up and words of reconciliation and grace are able to be said. And a good death is one where others also accept what is happening and are able to allow it, accept it, and support it.

Accidental and sudden deaths are tragic in that there often is not time for these things to occur. The natural physical, emotional and spiritual process is thwarted. This is a sad death. But when someone dies who will inevitably die, whether it be "before their time" or as a result of causes out of our control, that does not have to be a *bad death*.

In the case of persons like Jobs, I don't believe we ennoble them by making them into defeated heroes because they died of a disease. Jobs died. Of a disease. What happened to him, whilst undoubtedly unpleasant, was not unusual, peculiar or unnatural. Dying of cancer isn't heroic, and we must stop this incessant hero-making process when it comes to cancer. What makes a person a hero is what they were able to do with their humanity while they were alive, not their mortality. In fact, I believe we diminish the life of a person by making their mortal illness and death into some kind of act which might overshadow the things they were able to achieve in life.

I think we give cancer way too much credit when we say someone "lost their battle". Cancer didn't win. The cancer died when they died – how did it win? Because it caused their death?

Was the sum of their life diminished because their death was caused by cancer? Not one bit.

"Fighting" is not the default position of all people who have cancer. Being "beaten" is not the default position of all people who die from it. Most people with cancer die because of their vanquished bodies, not because of their vanquished souls. In the case of a great and successful man like Jobs, I think it's time we simply said, "He may have died because of cancer, but he fully lived whilst his body allowed." That, I believe, would be as fitting an epitaph as anyone could want.

39

The Disingenuous Doctrine Of God's Perfect Will –

Why Your Failure Doesn't Ruin His Reputation

Just a few years ago, I had no idea what Gods *perfect will for my life* was. Like most Christians, I prayed about it a lot. I listened to sermons on it in church, and read books about how to find out what it was. One thing I do know, actually trying to do Gods will is *really confusing*.

It's the whole *waiting on God* thing that does my head in. You know what you'd like to do, all indicators point to you needing to do this thing, but everyone says *oh, just wait on God*. Which is a Christian way of saying *don't rush it. Because you might fail, and then God will get a bad reputation.*

Because failing at something is the worst thing a Christian can do.

Hm. I happen to think there's two kinds of failure. There's the failure you get when what you tried to do doesn't work. And then there's the failure you get when you don't try in the first place.

I know why Christians say its way better to wait and see what God might do supernaturally than it is to just do something about it themselves. Its because we've believed if we rush in to take control, and things go wrong, someone will have to be held responsible for the failure. And God must never be blamed when things go wrong, because God is the God of *rightness, perfection and success*. Things must always turn out well, because Success = God was in it, Failure = God wasn't. And getting what you want, albeit by whatever spiritual-passive aggressive methods you prefer, definitely indicates that God was involved in the whole thing from woe to go. Failure means you must have done whatever it was via this weird thing called *in your own strength*.

I don't know what that phrase even means anymore. Christians use it a lot, but it's so ambiguous that it can mean anything from finding your own parking space to deciding whether or not to have chemotherapy. *Oh, don't even try to fight cancer/have a baby/enter into ministry/publish your book/find a partner/get a new job/change your abusive husband/give up your addiction in your own strength, just let God do it.* Hmmm.

Funny thing is, I have seen God do all these things. And in every instance, He used other people using their own strength helping the first person with the problem when He did them. Sometimes He actually had to, because the person with the problem refused to do anything about it themselves. They were too afraid of being accused of *doing it in their own strength.*

Is doing something *in our own strength* really something bad? Is using our own intelligence, physical resources or capacity really the *opposite* to God using His? What if our intelligence, physical resources and capacity, and Gods, are actually *the same thing*?

What this all boils down to is the fact that a lot Christians still believe the worst thing that can happen to them is failure. What is failure? Anything you said God told you to do that didn't happen. It's better to *wait on God to do it supernaturally*, and for nothing to ever happen at all, than to try and make something happen only to have it fall apart. Then, if nothing happens, we can attribute that to Gods will, and say He didn't want it to happen in the first place. It's not our fault. And we can't be accused of failing. *Phew.*

Small print - *because we never actually tried.*

Look, I'm all for the supernatural, and I believe in miracles. Point in case - a few years ago, my husbands business failed and we were $20,000 in debt. We both prayed that God would help us, *and that was a lot of praying, right there*. We worked for a year to satisfy the creditors, in our own strength, and managed to repay half the debt. Then one day, God gave us the other $10,000. Gave it to us. Well, when I say He gave it to us, I had to do something to go get it. Here's what happened.

One morning I got up and had an urge to take the dog for a walk on the beach. It was raining. *Go*, said God. OK, I said. I put the dog's leash on and started walking. *Not that way*, said God, *go the other way*. But it's further. *Just go*, said God. OK, I said. I got the to beach, in the rain, and started walking in the direction I usually did. *Not that way*, said God, *go the other way*. You must be joking, I said. *Just do it*, said God. As I walked up the beach in the opposite direction to the way I usually went, I looked down and saw something unusual. Unusual, but strangely familiar. *Pick that up*, said God, *pick that up, and take it home. That right there is exactly what you think it is.*

What was it? A huge lump of ambergris. It took me a couple of months, but eventually I sold it to the highest bidder - for $10,000.

Hilarious, don't you think, that God helped us, not by having someone forgive our debt, or write us an anonymous cheque - but by giving us a piece of dried up old vomit? Did we fail, well, *yeah*. Did He help us? He sure did. Did we wait around sulking until then? *Heck no*. We paid off $10,000 at $200 a week, which was 20% of our combined income. And we were committed to paying the lot back that way. Did God decide to cut us a break because we were willing to do whatever it took? I have no idea. I do know that when I told the man I sold the ambergris to, that I considered my finding it was a miracle from God, he just kept right on counting out my cash and answered drily, "Yeah, I   hear that a lot."

God lets us do things *in our own strength,* and He doesn't get mad when we do. After all, what on earth does He have to lose? Doing things in our own strength makes us *strong*. God also lets us make mistakes, and doesn't mind when we fail, because it makes us *wise*. God also lets us do things that may or may not be His will, because that makes us *interesting*. God wants us to be strong, wise and interesting, because when you think about it, that would mean we are just like Him. And God knows - literally - how much we're always rabbiting on about *that*.

When it comes to choices, decisions and consequences don't worry so much about this weird, passive-aggressive idea of Gods will. A very wise person once said to me that Gods will isn't like a cattle chute a cow is forced to shuttle down - it's like the huge, green paddock that she grazes in. Great advice. Loosen up. Have a go. Two things - just listen, He's speaking. And stay alive - you're not much good to anyone dead. Otherwise, go for it. What do you have to lose?

I know what God's will for my life is now. It's *to be alive*. To be alive means to sometimes fail, sometimes be hurt and sometimes fall down. Staying safe and getting things right, trying to keep to narrow idea of existential perfection isn't being alive - it's something else. Maybe madness. Maybe even death. My advice? Don't be afraid to make mistakes, to fail, to try things out, because more than he wants you to be safe, perfect or right, God wants you to be strong, smart and infinitely interesting, because funnily enough, that would make you exactly like Him.

40

Why Jesus Doesn't Want Your Smooshy Love

There's no doubt in most Christians minds that that Jesus was - and is - the kind of guy that just loves people to bits. After all, according to John 3:16, He did die on the cross for our redemption. A heck of a lot of people love Jesus right back too, and rightly so. After all, Jesus is not just the savior of mankind, He was pretty amazing as a human being, too. It's fully appropriate that we regard, respect and admire Jesus, as we do all the amazing people we know of, especially ones who do great things for us personally, and for the collective good of mankind. But there's something weird going on with Christians these days, particularly Christian women. It seems it's no longer enough to love Jesus Christ as God, as a great person, as a savior, a brother, or a friend. People - men and women - are *falling in love* with Jesus. That's *falling in love, romantically* - like they do in movies, like you do with your first crush, like you do with your boyfriend or girlfriend, husband or wife, like with Johnny Depp or Orlando Bloom or Aragorn. Christians are falling in love with Jesus - and encouraging others to do the same - just like teens at a Twilight movie. Like swooning fans of Justin Beiber and his ilk, they're falling for Jesus in churches and gatherings everywhere, quickly, obsessively, and sometimes even with a

231

great big mob of their screaming friends.

Am I the only person who isn't totally comfortable with this?

This is actually a *veeeeery* sensitive topic for me to broach. Many of my dearest friends enjoy what seem to be deeply intimate and even romantic relationships with the person of Jesus Christ, and I have no wish to criticise or alienate them. But I don't share their feelings, and the whole *falling in love with Jesus* thing just makes me feel very uncomfortable. I've tried to do it, and I've been strenuously encouraged - by the usual methods - socialisation, sermon, and song - to push my relationship with Christ to it's utmost emotional and spiritual limits, for as long as I can remember. But after all these years loving Christ and being loved back, I think I've found those limits, and they've stopped way before I could ever consider myself to be *in love* with Jesus. I consider Him my brother, my friend, my master and my Lord. But my *lover*?

Ew.

You see - I already have a lover. His name is Ben. I married him 23 years ago, and we have four children together. We've had our troubles, but at this time we are more in love than ever we have been. God gave us to each other, we believe, and we seek His help and guidance in our marriage every day. And we enjoy a level of physical intimacy with one another we don't share with anyone else. This love we have is God-ordained, and absolutely appropriate. The Bible describes this love in Greek as *eros* - sexy love - and according to the Bible it's for the enjoyment of people who are married to each other.

Ben is also my friend. We've been friends for a little longer than we've been married, and we are best friends. Literally, *best friends*. I don't have a female best friend - I gave them up a few years ago. Female best friend making and keeping caused so many problems in my marriage, I stopped trying to keep Ben and the female best friends, and decided just to keep the one friend I promised to love forever in front of God and everyone. I have a lot of friends, people I love, admire, respect and have history with, and like my marriage, this is a God-ordained kind of love. The Greek word is *philio* - brotherly love. I love my husband as my friend and brother in Christ, and he does the same for me. I also love my male and female friends that way, and this is entirely as it should be.

I have these other people in my life I love better than friends, but not in the same way I love Ben. My family - my parents, my children and my biological brothers. The Greek word for this is *storge* - familial love.

The other kind of love - one the Bible talks about in relation to God and us - is *agape*. Agape love is selfless, sacrificial, unconditional - and it's the love God has for us. This is the most difficult kind of love to practice, because it cuts the strings of expectation and obligation and just gives itself to its object expecting nothing in return. I try to love people with agape - and we're all encouraged as Christians and worshippers of God to love others as God loves us - but I'm not very good at it. Agape is God's special kind of love, and it's a miracle working kind of love. In fact, the only miracles I have ever seen or known of are the ones where agape love was practiced or experienced in its simplest and purest form.

In church, as far back as the eighties, congregations have been encouraged to fall in love with Jesus. I recall songs we sang, such as *I Keep Falling In Love With Him, Jesus - Lover Of My Soul* and *Falling In Love With Jesus,* and I know they made me squirm a little. We used to sing this song that went *Jesus, you have stolen my heart, I'm captivated by you,* and I just couldn't bring myself to sing it. I tried, but to be honest, it just felt weird talking about Him this way. I used to sing, *Jesus, you have all of my heart,* but even that seemed off, and was actually quite untrue. Jesus didn't have all of my heart, hadn't stolen the part He did have, and I wondered why we needed to use these images to describe what was meant to be the most natural, healthy thing for me to do in the world - have a relationship with Christ, and love the people He gave me to.

Besides, I didn't want to see Jesus as someone I could just *fall in love* with.

I didn't want my relationship with Christ to descend into the kind of emotional quagmire other romantic obsessions had in my past. And really, that's what falling in love means, isn't it? *Romantic obsession*. I don't know about you, but all my romantic obsessions had the following features. 1) They were based on an unrealistic picture of the person I was obsessed by 2) They sprang and were perpetuated from a place of deep unmet needs in me that actually needed to remain unmet for the obsession to continue, and I think they call that *co-dependance* 3) They inevitably ended badly, but always ended, because that kind of heightened emotional lust is simply not able to be satisfied, isn't in any way sustainable, and most certainly is not healthy.

There's another thing. The biggest problem I have with imagining myself to be *in love* with Jesus is the *imagining* part. *Falling in love* as a rule relies very, very heavily not on the wisdom, the will or the character of either of the lover or the loved - but on boundary breaking, fantasy and false expectation.

Do you really think Jesus wants us to do this? *For Him*?

I believe Christ loves me with *philio* love - I am certainly His friend. I also believe He loves me with what the Greeks called *storge* love - I am His sister, too. I have no trouble believing He loves me with *agape* love - His sacrificial love for me is evidenced in His actions on the cross on my behalf. But do I believe Christ wants me to express, feel or encourage anything other than these kinds of love toward Him?

I think when it comes to worshipping Christ, contemporary Christianity has kind of lost the plot. Instead of teaching reverence and the art of relationship, because that's all far too traditional and pedestrian and not very sexy, we've instead created a physical and spiritual celebrity of Jesus Christ and then made ourselves into His silly, screaming fans. We imagine Jesus as our doe-eyed boyfriend and cast Him in our imaginations as a youthful, chisel-featured and ever-chaste lover. We then paint ourselves in the role of perky-breasted ingénue in some broody teen movie based on Song of Solomon. But despite the fact the Bible describes Christ returning for His bride - the Church - that bride isn't literally *us, as individuals, as lovers*. Jesus doesn't want to be our boyfriend. He doesn't want to be our lover, in the sensual, sexual or erotic sense, at all. Call me old fashioned, but the more I get to know Him, the more I know He has no interest in sweeping me off my feet. Sorry, but that swoony Jesus movie you and He star in is all in your head. All the romantic notions of *falling in love* simply go against everything Jesus ever said or did when He was here, and everything that was said about Him before He came, and after He left.

I actually think the depiction of Jesus as a romantic object detracts from our relationships with real people, and teaches us to remain spiritually and emotionally immature. I don't want the kind of relationship in my imagination I have with my real-life husband. It feels *erky*. God gave me a husband made of flesh for a reason. Because I am made of flesh. I don't want to be chasing after an imaginary, pin-up Jesus when I have a real life Ben and a ring on my finger.

I know we've been told that loving our spouses and families and friends must come second to loving Jesus. For me, I find there's just no competition between them. In order for a competition to exist, I would have to shift Jesus Christ away from the God/Deity department in my head, and move Him across to the other part with the beings who won't clean the toilet after themselves and who look funny naked. Maybe your head doesn't work like that, but I suspect it does, and I happen to think loving Jesus and James Patterson with the same part of you is going to mess you up big time.

Jesus is not your boyfriend, and - male or female - I don't think you should try to fall in love with Him. If you don't have a part of you that can feel loved without needing to be pashed, pined over or pursued, you need to do some work on that. We were made to worship God, but worship is not what the world has taught us it is. It's not appropriate to love God like a celebrity, a pop star, or that unattainable sex-god you drooled over at high school. God's love is pure, and unlike romantic love, wants nothing from you. It cannot disappoint you. Your brother, friend and saviour Jesus Christ has transcended all that gushy, pop-star stuff, and what He has to offer you is vastly more interesting than anything you can think up, even in the most vivid imagination.

The final word, from the best-known scripture on love.

"When I was a child, I spoke and thought and reasoned as a child. But when I grew up, I put away childish things.

Now we see things imperfectly, like puzzling reflections in a mirror, but then we will see everything with perfect clarity. All that I know now is partial and incomplete, but then I will know everything completely, just as God now knows me completely.

Three things will last forever--faith, hope, and love--and the greatest of these is love." 1 Corinthians 13: 11 - 13

41

Surprising Things I've Learned Are True

Since I Stopped Going To Church

I've been thirty years a Christian, and about twenty-five of those involved in church in one way or another. I know some stuff about church, and a lot more the last few years, since we stopped going to church so much. Here is what I once kind of suspected was true, and now, know for sure.

It's impossible to have all the answers. Funny, that. And you know what? Nobody outside the church really expects you to have them all anyway. Sure, there are your argumentative types, but you'll find most of them are other Christians. I know we've been told we need to be able to give a thorough and theologically accurate answer to anyone who challenges us, but in my experience, people who don't go to church seldom actually ask for one. Anne Lamott once wrote, and I've found it to be true, how a friend of hers said that most people just want the answer to two questions - 1) Who's in charge around here? 2) How much do you love me? When it comes to people, I think that's all you really need to know. Most unchurched people I know respond with warmth and relief when a Christian says to them politely and   sincerely, "I don't know."

It's natural and okay not to get along with everyone. God is love, and *a friend loves at all times* and all that, but you and I both know sometimes it's just *impossible*. Let's just call a spade a spade - some people you just get along with better than others, and that's perfectly fine. There are people in this world you will never have anything in common with, or be friends with, or even be able to be in the same room with, and that's just the way it is. I know we've been taught we must be friendly and compliant and cheerful and sweet to everyone we come across, but lets face it, even Jesus was mighty pissed off at times, and sometimes with his own friends. Cut yourself some slack. Not everyone you clash with isn't your friend, and not everyone who is nice to you is. Boy - ain't *that* the truth.

God doesn't always make things work out in the end. This is sometimes the hardest thing for believers to accept, but the reality is sometimes people pray about things and get what they want, and sometimes they pray and believe and they don't get what they want. Sometimes people pray for healing, and the person they prayed for actually dies. And sometimes nobody prays, and nobody even believes in God in the first place, and everything works out just great. This is the way of the world. Keep on praying that things will go well, but also accept that part of them going well is you being contented with whatever outcome comes to pass. It's the prayer and the faith in itself that is the victory, not getting what it was you prayed and believed for in the first place.

People who aren't Christians usually know exactly what they're doing. I know we've been told that all non-Christians are hard-hearted and ignorant. I know we've been told everyone who doesn't share our faith is uninformed, and misinformed, and has been led astray. I know we've been told they are all dead in their sins and blind to the truth, and will always be naturally opposed to everything you or I as a Christian say and represent. But you should know that non-Christians are not as selfish and stupid and pig-headed as we have presumed. You should know that people who are not Christians actually do you a great service by allowing you to practice your religion freely in their midst, and sometimes even in their face in quite a patronising fashion. You should be grateful that many non-religious persons vehemently defend your right to worship your god whenever and however you want to, despite the fact there is no benefit in it for them, other than they wish to live in a society where this is possible. Christians also ought to thank God that the people we may have considered dead in their sins do not consider our Christianity a crime or an offence, and we also ought to honour the fact that un-Christian law makers have written into legislation your right to profess and practice our faith, and are happy to benefit from our input into society because of our moral right-standing.

Universities and parliaments and hospitals are filled with people who have given their lives to help and govern and educate people just like us, regardless of our opinion of them or our high-minded views about their religion, or lack of it. Our society's education, health and freedom is facilitated by the service and leadership of these whom Christians often consider to be ignorant and immoral, and we do well to give due respect. It does not behoove Christians to hold onto the collective mindset that presumes acceptance of Christ is the peak of human intelligence and sophistication. Because we would be wrong about that. Respect and regard for other human beings however may turn out to be.

***The way we do things* here isn't compulsory.** Of all the things that surprised me when I no longer was part of a church, this surprised me the most. You can really do whatever *you* want, judge, think or decide, and the world does not come to an end. All your friends do not have to agree, participate or confer.

Some churches love this part - the part that says *this is the way we do things here* - so much, they have a name for it - *church culture*. It's what makes us feel we belong to something bigger than ourselves, and gives us reassurance that given the same set of circumstances, others would do what we've chosen to do. But church culture can be very constraining, and even damaging. It separates us from those outside the church, but also from each other. Church culture defines not only what choices we make, but perhaps even what we wear and how we talk. It may dictate what we do, and affect our decision making. Thus, the person who chooses a divorce, or who accepts their child's homosexuality, or even who simply takes a job with hours that restrict church participation may be subject to intense disapproval from their congregational peers. Observers then watch and learn that they should never dare to do the same. The *right thing* is *the way we do things here*, and vice versa. I have found though that the very people who like to help you choose *the right thing* are seldom there to help in the same way when that *right thing* goes to hell in a hand-basket. While we ought to seek wise counsel, we ought never, ever lose our strength in deciding for ourselves. You alone will bear the consequences of your actions.

Working for/in/with the church won't solve all your other problems. Once, a friend of mine who was having terrible marriage problems was told *now honey, just devote yourself to the life of the church, and God will sort out all your problems for you*. He didn't. In all my thirty years as a Christian, I've yet to see this happen. When my own marriage fell apart, one of the issues I actually had to work through was my absolute, pig-headed determination over the years to remain involved in church life and activities regardless of the things that were happening in our relationship, and to our family. I have now turned my complete attention away from being a worship leader in the church and servicing it's needs to being a wife, and working on my own marriage as a ongoing concern. There are Godly priorities, and there are Godly priorities.

If you give the church your money, the church gets your money. I can't be any more blunt. If you give your money to the church, the church will spend it. As they see fit. They may give it to missionaries, or they may use it to pay the electricity bill on their five hundred-seat auditorium. They may use it for the salaries of the pastors, or they may sink it into investments you have no way of knowing about or endorsing. They may use it to expand God's kingdom on earth, or they may fritter it away on stupid things and even lose it forever. If you give your money to the church, you can call it tithing or offerings or whatever the heck you want, but if you give it to the church, the church gets your money. It's not spiritual, metaphysical supernatural or existential in any way, shape or form. As long as you don't have a problem with that, then there's no problem with you giving your money to the church.

The church is there to help you, but only sometimes. I do not mean this unkindly. There are certain problems the church will be happy to help you with, and others they will not be so keen to get involved with. Here's a clue - if there is any possible way the outcome will preserve God's good reputation, they'll probably want to help you out. If it could all go terribly wrong, and probably will, or won't be something you will be likely to give a positive testimony about afterwards, you better find another way of solving the problem. When I had cancer, the church was falling over themselves to help me. When it turned out that my husband had become mentally ill, an alcoholic and lost his business and all our money, it was a different story. The church loves victims. Perpetrators? Not so much.

You'll never be in the "in" crowd. If I have learned anything, I have learned this. I know it looks like there is an *in-crowd* at your church. I know there seems to be an inner echelon, a tight-knit circle of the elect, chosen ones that everyone on the outside looks up to. I know it seems like there is a master race of ministers at the top, and everybody wants to be them, or be with them, or be just like them. But there isn't. I know you've asked them and they've said there isn't, and you haven't believed them, but take my word for it, it's true. They are just like you, except their mortgage documents read "minister of religion." Next time you feel like envying them, think about that.

You know how you feel insecure sometimes about your life, and have doubts about your faith? So do they. You know how you feel stupid and ugly and dirty and unloved and rejected and like nobody would ever be your friend if they knew what you were really like? Those people you look up to feel that way too. There is no *dream team*, no inner circle, no in-club

245

of ones who have *made it* in ministry life. They sure don't think they are any better than you, in fact, they know full well they are exactly like you in every way that matters.

Those people in church you look up to might seem more confident, more capable and more anointed, but they aren't, in reality, or in their minds. Don't resume their arrogance just because they have "made it" into ministry. Trust me. Those people you idolise feel just as intimidated and insecure as you do, and they know they are nothing special. They know all they have going for them is God's grace, so don't you go thinking they have anything else, over and above what you have, okay? Pastors and leaders know full well they are called not just to lead, but also to *serve*, and for the most part, they take it very seriously, and with humility. Being a pastor is one of the hardest jobs I can imagine.

Church isn't meant to replace your brain or your personality, but many people still act like it is. We are the church, and it should reflect everything that we are - mind, soul, personality, character. We are flawed - the church will be too. We are less than - the church will be too. We are trying to be better - the church will be too. We are redeemed by grace - and the church is this too. The church does not replace our intelligence, our diversity, our judgment or our humanity - it is the expression of these. Hold on to everything you are - the church needs it all, the world needs it all. God needs it all. After all, He made you in His image. For God's sake - don't let anyone unmake you in theirs.

When Your Love Language Seems To Be All Four Letter Words

On days like today, I think back to about fifteen years ago when those Love
Language books were all the rage for married couples and parents. We just
ate those books up, all desperate to learn the unspoken cry of our loved
ones heart, and unravel the mystery of why we all act the way we do, when
all we really want is love. According to the author of the books, there are
five love languages - words of affirmation, physical touch, quality time,
receiving gifts and acts of service - and each one of these is a conduit
through which we "feel" the love of others, and prefer to give it in return.
Learning our loved one's love language is apparently a bit like turning the
key of their heart, leading us toward closer and more fulfilling
relationships.

Now, I'm a very pragmatic kind of person. I always had a bit of trouble
remembering what the five love languages were, let alone applying them to
different people. I would forget that I was supposed to spend quality time
with this one, buy that one a sweet and thoughtful gift, and always mind
that I said something kind and affirming to the other one. I found it
difficult to remember these things not because I was indifferent to my kids

needs, but because my own love language was simplicity, structure and *total and ultimate control of everything*. Just give me your complete and unbending compliance, and keep it simple, stupid, cried the unspoken voice of my heart, and everything around here will be *just fine*.

Problem is, kids will have their love languages whether we their parents heed them or not. And because I did remember from time to time my children actually owed me nothing - including their mindless obedience - over time, my love language lost quite a few phrases from its vocabulary. "Or else" was one. "Because I said so." was another. "Would you like me to pull this car over and give you a spanking?" went away round about the time I realised being spanked didn't fit into *any* of Mr. Chapmans real love languages, and wasn't actually working for me or our kids anyway.

Anyway, days like today make me think about those five love languages, how sometimes the things we do don't really fit into any of those categories, and how someone needs to tell that to the teenage person living here and make her *get with the program*. Otherwise I may have to bring back some of my lost vocabulary, especially the part about the spanking.

I've decided that when it comes to the mysterious ways of teenagers, five love languages aren't nearly enough. Because the things they do can be just so incredibly baffling at times I think there definitely needs to be a few new ones, and I've had a stab - not a word I feel comfortable toying with today, after the morning I've had with my teen - at creating a few categories of my own.

1) **What's mine is mine - what's yours is mine.** This morning, as I prepared to drive my teen to work, I detected a familiar scent wafting through the car. It was my expensive perfume - a gift from my husband. I, however, wasn't the one wearing it. "Have you run out of perfume?" I asked, puzzled, as last I looked this individual had two bottles of scent on her own dressing table. "No." And that was the only explanation offered. Later, the same teen walked past my bedroom door announcing, "I'm going for ride." Interesting. She doesn't own a bike. "A ride?" I asked? A head appeared in my doorway, wearing my bike helmet. "Yes." This particular love language expressed once in a day? I could perhaps graciously relent. Twice in a twenty-four hour period? Both grace and surrender are abandoned. Lucky she was wearing a helmet.

2) **Don't speak to me, just take me where I need to go**. Teens reserve the right to maintain objectionable silence whilst consecutively enjoying the benefit of being transported wherever they wish to go, often at a moments notice, and without the offer of contribution, financial or otherwise. But that's okay, really. Because they didn't ask to be born,

and being alive and seventeen is *so hard*. No, really it is - I remember.

3) **I am beautiful, I am hideous**. I hate this one the most, because it is sheer torture for the darling individual who must endure it, and for the loving family who must witness it.

4) **You don't understand me, please listen to me.** I know she thinks I don't get it, and I know I think I do. I also know there's nothing I want more in this world than the pure trust she gives me when she finally lets me in.

5) **I abhor crass materialism in all its forms, so will *you* buy it for me instead?** Teens cannot abide attempts by parents to buy their affections with *things*, and similarly, many have denounced consumer culture and commercialism outright. But that doesn't apply to things they *need*, like mobile phones and festival tickets. In this case, spending a lot of money is perfectly okay. I have noticed that a teenager's income is theirs to spend as they please, and their parent's income is theirs to spend as they please too. Forget about Occupy Wall Street - to hear them tell it, *teenagers* are the 99%. And sometimes, as a parent, it certainly feels that way.

Five love languages are not enough. Ten are not enough. How many ways can a family give and receive love between them? There are not enough words, gestures, sacrifices or actions that can adequately express the deep complexities of relationship. Five? Try a hundred and twenty five. And all those love languages will not always be civil, or even comprehensible. Sometimes a love language can feel like it's all four-letter words. Sometimes a love language will be more a question than an answer, more a longing than a fulfillment, more a defining than a uniting. But that is the essence of relationship - not the answer or the conclusion that you come to about one another, but the process of discovery, discerning and of understanding traversed while coming to appreciate that they are not you, and nor would you have them be, no matter how much you want to keep them safe and close and happy.

And, for the record, I just want to say there was *nothing* about all this in the manual.

43

Good Girls Never Change The World

Of all the stories surrounding Jesus that appear in the Bible, one of my favourites would have to be the account in John chapter four of the Samaritan woman who speaks with Jesus at the well. Now, I've heard many readings of this passage, most which focus entirely on Jesus' words and actions – mostly lauding His marvelous condescension at lowering himself to speak to a woman, and a Samaritan at that. I realise that it is indicative of Jesus' nature that he seemingly wasn't bound by sexist or racist conventions. But why are we so surprised? Why would he be bound by sexist or racist conventions?

Er, Son of God, people.

(Just as an aside, I'm trying to imagine what it would be like to be identified in your most defining moment throughout the ages not by your name, but instead by two words representing your ethnic group and your gender. "Hi everyone, you may know me as the 'Samaritan Woman', but my name is really Pamela Jones…")

No, I'm not surprised Jesus was prepared to speak to a Samaritan woman.

Jesus never was one for conventions. What I am surprised about is the fact that the Samaritan woman was prepared to speak to Jesus right back. Because women – especially Samaritan women – just didn't do that sort of thing. Not only did she speak with Jesus, at length, about theology (what was she thinking?), she went back to her town and told everyone there what they talked about. And as if it wasn't bad enough to fess up about having a private conversation with a Jewish rabbi – in private – in order to tell people about Jesus, she also had to blather quite a bit about herself. Not that they probably didn't already know of her shadowy past, but nevertheless, it was pretty brave of her to bring it up. In *public*. "I just met up with this man…(I can hear them – "Oh, *really*?")…who told me everything I ever did." she reports. Which part?

"I just met up with this man…." (I can just hear them – "*Oh, really?*") "….who told me everything I ever did." Which part? "Oh, just the part about me being married five times before, and how the guy I'm living with now isn't even my husband." Oops. Embarrassed much? Apparently not.

"Come see a man who told me everything I ever did." she insisted. *Come on!* Don't hassle me now with all that living-in-sin crap. *Come and see him!*

Come meet the guy who read me like a book. Come see the man who exposed my shameful actions and didn't flinch. Come listen to the rabbi who shouldn't have spoken to me, but who did, and to whom I spoke back. Funny thing is, they did come. And the Bible says that "many of the Samaritans from that town believed in him because of the woman's testimony, 'He told me everything I ever did.'" The Samaritans went off and sought Jesus out, and had him come stay with them for a few days so they could learn more. And because of that, many more believed.

I love the Samaritan woman. She didn't have anything else to report except "I met Jesus, and he knew all my crap." That was all she had to say, and it was more than enough to bring the Way, the Truth and the Life to a people who would otherwise have avoided Jesus like the plague, and who would not have had a disciple come within a stones throw in a pink fit. Good for her. I guess that's why she's in the Bible – someone obviously thought what even with all the things she had done wrong, something the Samaritan woman did was very, very right.

44

God Can Take My Mental Illness –

Just Not The Part Where He Speaks To Me

I asked my husband this morning, "Do you think we'll ever go back to church?" After a few moments, he replied, "I'm not going back until God tells me to." "You do at least ask Him about it, don't you?" I asked. "Every day." said my man.

Now, I trust my husband. I haven't always, but we've been through an awful lot together, and I certainly do now. I know with confidence that he talks to God, and I know that God answers him back. I know a lot of people say they can't hear God's voice, and don't know when He's speaking to them. But my husband does, and I do too. We started hearing God speak to us very early on, and funnily enough, when we did what he asked us, He kept on speaking, and we kept hearing Him speak.

And amazing things have happened whenever He has spoken and we have listened.

Here's three life-changing examples of how God has spoken (we believe) undoubtedly, and directly to us. There have been others, but these are three of the best.

Ben and I dated briefly when I was 19 and he was 17, for three months. Then I fell pregnant. Oops. Obviously, we weren't up for listening to God much at that time. But thankfully, we both believed He was bigger than any of our stupid mistakes, and we asked Him what should we do. "***Have your baby, because that's going to be awesome, and get married, because I love families***." And that's exactly what we did. People were amazed we would even try it, but we were not afraid. God said it was going to be cool. Those two decisions changed our lives, and have been two of the best things we ever did. A few bumps along the way, we've been best friends and lovers for 23 years, and we have four amazing children.

Just a few years back, Ben found himself in big trouble. He had developed a drinking problem due to a terrible depression, a legacy of my having cancer a few years before. He was not a well man. His business suffered, and eventually, we went out backwards, owing tens of thousands of dollars. We prayed that God would help us, and started paying back our creditors a few hundred dollars a month at a time. It took us a year to pay back half of what we owed. Ben would drive to a lookout every morning before work and pray, "God, please help me get my family out of this mess." One day, I got out of bed and God clearly told me - despite the fact it was pouring rain - to take the dog for a walk on the beach. "***Just do it.***" He said. As I walked up the beach that morning, I found a piece of rare and extremely valuable ambergris (Google it, it's whale vomit, used in the perfume making process)- which I was able to sell for exactly the amount we needed to pay back the rest of our debt. The trader told me that our large piece had been floating around on the ocean for at least twenty years - the same age as our eldest son - until it washed up on the beach that day. These days, I always get out of bed when God says, *"Just do it."*

Even after we paid back Ben's debts, his drinking - and my inability to deal with it - slowly and surely destroyed our marriage. He went away to rehab, and I shook his hand at the gate and thanked him for some great years, and wished him a nice rest-of-his-life. I went home to try and finish raising our family alone, and he resigned himself to a six month rehabilitation program, and beyond that, well, who knows what. About three months into his program, the rehab coordinator asked to meet with me. "Ben's making progress," he said, "he is very sorry for what happened to the marriage." "Too little, too late." I said. "I am under no obligation to give that man a second chance. I don't think I could ever trust him again." The coordinator sat quietly while I made my case for why Ben could never, ever come home again. Then he said, "Oh, I agree. You are under no obligation to trust Ben. I think you should simply do what God tells you to do." What a thing to say to me. I asked God what I should do, and He said, *"Listen to*

Ben. Just listen. He has something to say to you. *"* I told Ben I was prepared to hear whatever he had to say to me. He didn't say much- he never has - but he did say that he knew he wanted to still be married to me. I said I'd think about it. I went away and got very angry with God. "I can't - I won't - forgive or trust that man again. I can't go back to living like that. How can I believe that he has changed?" And God said something to me I will never, ever forget. He said -

"Jo, I am a rewarder of those who diligently seek me. Ben has diligently sought me. And you are his reward."

Well, what would *you* do if God told you that?

And so, here we are. I can say truthfully that I trust my husband. And I *love* my husband. He listens to God, and I know he hears His voice. And Ben knows I do too. Our marriage - from its beginning, right through to now - is proof of that. God speaks. And what He says always makes sense, but also always requires we risk something, albeit sometimes just our pride. And I know we have never come out empty handed whenever we have taken that risk.

One day we will go back to church again, and it will be as big a risk as our obedience to His voice has been every other time. And when it happens, it won't be a moment too soon, or too   late.

THE END

Please visit my blog at

www.johilder.com

or contact me

mail@johilder.com

11012090R00146

Printed in Great Britain
by Amazon.co.uk, Ltd.,
Marston Gate.